Mister God, this is Anna

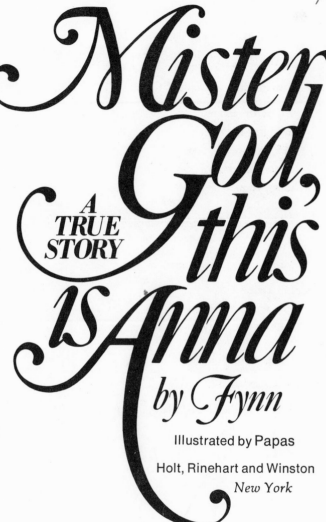

Mister God, this is Anna

A TRUE STORY

by Fynn

Illustrated by Papas

Holt, Rinehart and Winston
New York

Library of Congress Cataloging in Publication Data

Fynn.
Mister God, this is Anna.

I.   Title.
PZ4.F99Mi3 [PR6056.Y5]   823'.9'14   75–541
ISBN 0–03–014716–6

Designed by Robert Reed

First published in the United States in 1975

Printed in the United States of America

10 9 8 7 6 5 4 3

INTRODUCTION

The story of Anna is so strange and so enchanting that at first I found it difficult to believe it was about real people.

Anna was a little girl of four when Fynn, a young man of nineteen, found her late at night sitting outside a baker's shop in London's dockland. She had run away from her parents, who had been ill-treating her; her bruised body told the story. She was determined not to return to them and refused to say where she lived. Fynn took her home where his large-hearted mother took her into the family circle as one of her own. An unusual and moving friendship developed between the little girl and the big young man. He found her to be not only a delightful and interesting child, but a kind of infant prodigy, especially in God-thinking. She wrestled with profound theological issues in her own intuitive and reasonable way and expressed her findings in startlingly simple words. As Fynn writes, "Anna was not only deeply in love with Mister God, she was proud of him." The fact that she spoke the rough language of the street made her pronouncements all the more astonishing—sometimes breathtaking.

"A bomb with legs on" is how Fynn describes Anna. Indeed she seems such an unusual child that sometimes the reader may wonder—as I did when first confronted with the author's manuscript—whether she is not in fact a fictional character—a kind of "mini-myth"—invented by an adult of original and questing mind as the means of communicating thoughts about God in a new language. But I am convinced that Anna was a real little girl, who was in fact found in the streets at the age of four and who died as a result of an ugly fall at the age of seven.

The manuscript, just sixty pages of it, was brought into my office by a man who told us that the author was a friend of his and that it was most unlikely he would be willing to meet me. Those first sixty pages were enough for me to realize that the story of Anna was one of the most exceptional manuscripts that I had ever had the chance of publishing.

The problems that faced me were Who is the author? and Is this a story about real people? and How could I find out if the author refused to come to see me? At last, after long negotiations, he agreed to come.

Fynn arrived in a very bellicose mood. The reason he was reluctant to meet us was that Anna's death had been for him such a traumatic experience that thirty years had had to pass before he felt he could write about her. Anna was still so much a part of his life that he dreaded to expose her to what he thought would be the arrogant rough and tumble of a commercial publisher's editorial and publicity expertise.

After Anna's death, Fynn had suffered a nervous break-down. He is now a brilliant scientist and computer expert. Meeting him was a dramatic experience. Here in front of us was undoubtedly the Fynn one had met in the book—tall, handsome, sensitive, with an innocence and honesty that is rare to meet. In a matter of seconds I found that I was on the same wavelength and just sat back and listened to Fynn telling the story of Anna. I sent a brilliant editor to stay with Fynn and his wife in the country to discuss the many editorial problems that arose during the writing of the book. There was so much material to use, cutting was necessary so that Anna's character should not be hidden under a load of de-tails. Our editor loved his visits to Fynn. They talked far into the night. Our editor himself had worked in the East End some thirty years ago and he knew so well the scenes and atmosphere described by Fynn.

We were determined from the very start that Fynn should remain anonymous. He felt, and we agreed, that if he had to relive the story of Anna over and over again in interviews it would be very upsetting for him.

I have been asked, "Is the book genuine?" My reply is that I won't claim every word is verbatim. But the substance, mood, and atmosphere are authentic. In all my publishing ex-perience of over fifty years I have never handled such an amazing story.

William Collins
Chairman, Collins Publishers, London

ONE "The diffrense from a person and an angel is easy. Most of an angel is in the inside and most of a person is on the outside." These are the words of six-year-old Anna, sometimes called Mouse, Hum, or Joy. At five years, Anna knew absolutely the purpose of being, knew the meaning of love, and was a personal friend and helper of Mister God. At six, Anna was a theologian, mathematician, philosopher, poet, and gardener. If you asked her a question you would always get an answer—in due course. On some occasions the answer would be delayed for weeks or months; but eventually, in her own good time, the answer would come: direct, simple, and much to the point.

She never made eight years; she died by an accident. She died with a grin on her beautiful face. She died saying, "I bet Mister God lets me get into heaven for this." And I bet he did too.

I knew Anna for just about three and a half years. Some people lay claim to fame by being the first person to sail around the world alone, or to stand on the moon, or by some other act of bravery. All the world has heard of such people. Not many people have heard of me, but I, too, have a claim to fame; for I knew Anna. To me this was the high peak of adventure. This was no casual knowing; it required total application. For I knew her on her own terms, the way she demanded to be known: from the inside first. "Most of an angel is in the inside," and this is the way I learned to know her—my first angel. Since then I have learned to know two other angels, but that's another story.

My name is Fynn. Well that's not quite true; my real name doesn't matter all that much since my friends all called me Fynn and it stuck. If you know your Irish mythology you will know that Fynn was pretty big; me too.

Standing about six feet two, weighing some 225 pounds, close to being a fanatic on physical culture, the son of an Irish mother and a Welsh father, with a passion for hot dogs and chocolate raisins—not together, I may add. My great delight was to roam about dockland in the night-time, particularly if it was foggy.

My life with Anna began on such a night. I was nineteen at the time, prowling the streets and alleys with my usual supply of hot dogs, the street lights with their foggy halos showing dark formless shapes moving out from the darkness of the fog and disappearing again. Down the street a little way, a baker's shop window softened and warmed the raw night with its gas lamps. Sitting on the grating under the window was a little girl. In those days children wandering the streets at night were no uncommon sight. I had seen such things before, but on this occasion it was different. How or why it was different has long since been forgotten except that I am sure it was different. I sat down beside her on the grating, my back against the shop front. We stayed there about three hours. Looking back over thirty years, I can now cope with those three hours; but at the time I was on the verge of being destroyed. That November night was pure hell; my guts tied themselves into all manner of complicated knots.

Perhaps even then something of her angelic nature caught hold of me; I'm quite prepared to believe that I had been bewitched from the beginning. I sat down with "Shove up a bit, Tich." She shoved up a bit but made no comment.

"Have a hot dog," I said.

She shook her head and answered, "It's yours."

"I got plenty. Besides, I'm full up," I said.

She made no sign, so I put the bag on the grating between us. The light from the shop window wasn't very strong and the kid was sitting in the shadows so I couldn't see what she looked like except that she was very dirty. I could see that she clutched under one arm a rag doll and on her lap a battered old paint box.

We sat there for thirty minutes or so in complete silence; during that time I thought there had been a movement of her hand toward the hot dog bag but I didn't want to look or comment in case I put her off. Even now I can feel the immense pleasure I had when I heard the sound of that hot dog skin popping under the bite of her teeth. A minute or two later she took a second and then a third. I reached into my pocket and brought out a packet of Woodbines.

"Do you mind if I smoke while you're eating, Tich?" I asked.

"What?" She sounded a little alarmed.

"Can I have a cigarette while you're eating?"

She rolled over and got to her knees and looked me in the face.

"Why?" she said.

"My Mum's a stickler for politeness. Besides, you don't blow smoke in a lady's face when she's eating," I said.

She stared at half a hot dog for a moment or two, and looking at me fully, she said, "Why? Do you like me?"

I nodded.

"You have a cigarette then," and she smiled at me and popped the rest of the hot dog into her mouth.

I took out a Woodbine and lit up and offered her the match to blow out. She blew, and I was sprayed with bits of hot dog. This little accident produced such a reaction in her that I felt that I had been stabbed in the guts. I had seen a dog cringe before, but never a child. The look she gave me filled me with horror. She expected a thrashing. She clenched her teeth as she waited for me to strike her.

3

What my face registered I don't know, perhaps anger and violence, or shock and confusion. Whatever it was, it produced from her the most piteous whimper. I can't describe this sound after all these years; no words are fitting. The feeling I can still taste, can still experience. My heart faltered at the sound, and something came undone inside me. My clenched fist hit the pavement beside me, a useless gesture in response to Anna's fears. Did I think of that image then, that image which I now think of, the only one that fits the occasion? That perfection of violence, that ultimate horror and bewilderment of Christ crucified. That terrible sound that the child made was a sound that I never wish to hear again. It attacked my emotional being and blew a fuse.

After a moment or two I laughed. I suppose that the human mind can only stand so much grief and anguish. After that, the fuses blow. With me, the fuses blew in a big way. The next few minutes I know very little about—except that I laughed and laughed. Then I realized that the kid was laughing too. No shrunken bundle of fear—she was laughing. Kneeling on the pavement and leaning forward with her face close to mine, and laughing—laughing. So very many times in the next three years I heard her laughter—no silver bells or sweet rippling sounds was her laughter, but like a five-year-old's bellow of delight, a cross between a puppy's yelp, a motorbike, and a bicycle pump.

I put my hands on her shoulders and held her off at arm's length, and then came that look that is entirely Anna's—mouth wide open, eyes popping out of her head, like a whippet straining at the leash. Every fiber of that little body was vibrating and making a delicious sound. Legs and arms, toes and fingers, the whole of that little

body shook and trembled like Mother Earth giving birth
to a volcano. And what a volcano was released in that
child!

Outside that baker's shop in dockland on a foggy November night I had the unusual experience of seeing a
child born. After the laughter had quieted off a bit, but
while her little body was still thrumming like a violin
string, she tried to say something, but it wouldn't come
out properly. She managed a "You—You—You—."

After some little time and a great deal of effort she
managed, "You love me, don't you?"

Even had it not been true, I could not have said no to
save my life; true or false, right or wrong, there was only
one answer. I said yes.

She gave a little giggle, and pointing a finger at me, said, "You love me," and then broke into some primitive gyration around the lamppost, chanting, "You love me. You love me. You love me."

Five minutes of this and she came back and sat down on the grating. "It's nice and warm for your bum, ain't it?" she said.

I agreed it was nice for your bum.

A moment later: "I ain't arf firsty." So we upped and went along to the pub just down the road. I bought a large bottle of stout. She wanted "one of them ginger pops with the marble in the neck." So she had two ginger pops and some more hot dogs from an all-night coffee stall.

"Let's go back and get our bums warm again," she grinned at me. Back we went and sat on the grating, a big un and a little un.

I don't suppose that we drank more than a half of the drinks, for it seemed that the idea of a fizzy drink was to shake it vigorously and then let it shoot up into the air. After a few showers of ginger pop and a determined effort to do the nose trick, she said, "Now do it to yourn."

I'm sure even then that this was not a request but an order. I shook hard and long and then let fly with the stopper and we both were covered with frothy stout.

The next hour was filled with giggles and hot dogs, ginger pop and chocolate raisins. The occasional passerby was yelled at: "Oi, Mister, he loves me, he do." Running up the steps of a nearby building she shouted, "Look at me. I'm bigger than you."

About ten-thirty that evening, while she was sitting between my knees having an earnest conversation with Maggie, her rag doll, I said, "Come on, Tich, it's about time you were in bed. Where do you live?"

6

In a flat, matter-of-fact voice she exclaimed, "I don't live nowhere. I have runned away."

"What about your mum and dad?" I asked.

She might have said the grass is green and the sky is blue. What she did say was just as factual and effortless. "Oh, she's a cow and he's a sod. And I ain't going to no bleeding cop shop. I'm going to live with you."

This was no request but an order. What could you do? I merely accepted the fact. "Right, I agree. You can come home with me and then we will have to see."

At that point my education began in earnest. I'd got myself a large doll, but not an imitation doll, a real live one, and from what I could make out, a bomb with legs on. Going home that night was like coming home from Hampstead Heath, slightly drunk, a little dizzy from the merry-go-round I'd been on, and not a little bewildered that the beautiful doll I'd won on the shooting range had come to life and was walking beside me.

"What's your name, Tich?" I asked her.

"Anna. What's yours?"

"Fynn," I said. "Where do you come from?"

I didn't get an answer to this question, and that was the first and last time she didn't answer a question; I gathered later the reason for this. It was because she was afraid that I might have taken her back.

"When did you run away?"

"Oh, three days ago, I think."

We took the short way home by climbing over the railway bridge and crossing the train yards. This was always my way in because we lived next to the railway and it was convenient, to say nothing of the fact that it meant I didn't have to get Mum out of bed to open the front door.

We got into the scullery by the back door and then into the kitchen. I lit the gas. For the very first time I saw

7

Anna. God only knows what I expected to see; certainly not what I did see. It wasn't that she was dirty or that her frock was about ten sizes too big; it was the mixture of ginger pop, stout, and her paint tin. She looked like a little savage, smears of various colored paints all over her face and arms, the front of her frock a complete riot of color. She looked so funny and so tiny, and her response to my bellow of laughter so reduced her to her cowering self again, that I hurriedly picked her up to the level of the mirror over the mantelpiece and made her look. Her delicious little giggle was like closing the door on November and stepping out into June. I can't say that I looked much different that night. I too was covered in paint. "A right pair," as Mum later said.

In the middle of all the giggles there was a *thump, thump, thump* on the wall. That was Mum's signal. "That you? Your supper's in the oven and don't forget to turn the gas off."

Instead of the usual "OK, Mum, won't be long," this night I opened the door and yelled down the passage, "Mum, come and see what I've got."

One thing about Mum, she was never fussed about anything; she took everything in her stride. Bossy, the cat I brought home one night, and Patch the dog, eighteen-year-old Carol, who stayed with us for two years, and Danny from Canada, who stayed about three years. Some people collect stamps or beer mats; Mum collected waifs and strays, cats, dogs, frogs, people, and as she believed, a whole host of "little people." Had she been confronted that night with a lion, she'd have made the same comment—"The poor thing." One look when she came through the door was enough. "The poor thing," she cried, "what have they done to you?" And then, as an afterthought, to me, "You look a right mess. Wash your face." With that, Mum flopped onto her knees and put her arms around Anna.

Being embraced by Mum was like tangling with a gorilla. Mum had arms like other people have legs. Mum had a unique anatomical structure which still puzzles me, for she had a 200-pound heart in a 170-pound body. Mum was a real lady and wherever she may be now, she'll still be a lady.

A few minutes of "ooh's" and "aah's," then things began to get organized. Mum heaved herself upright, and with a passing shot to me to "get those wet clothes off the child," flung open the kitchen door, yelling, "Stan, Carol, come here quick!" Stan's my younger brother by two years; Carol was one of the waifs or strays that came and went.

The kitchen and the scullery suddenly erupted—a bath appeared, kettles of water on gas rings, towels, soap; the kitchen range was filled with coal, and there was me, trying to undo sundry hooks and eyes on Anna's clothing. And suddenly there she was, sitting cross-legged on the table as raw as the day she was born. Stan said, "Bastard!" Carol said, "Christ!" Mum looked a bit grim. For a moment that little kitchen blazed with hatred for someone; that poor little body was bruised and sore. The four older people in the kitchen were ready to bash someone, and for a time we were lost in our own anger. But Anna sat and grinned, a huge face-splitting grin. Like some beautiful sprite she sat there, and I believe for the very first time in her life she was entirely and completely happy.

The bath completed, the soup downed, and Anna resplendent in Stan's old shirt, we all sat around the kitchen table and took stock of the situation. Questions were asked but no answers were forthcoming. We eventually decided that the day had had enough questions asked. The

9

answers could wait until tomorrow. While Mum went to work getting Anna's clothes clean again, Stan and I made up a bed on an old black leather sofa next door to me.

I slept in the front room, a room stuffed full of aspidistras, a tallboy with the precious pieces of cut glass displayed on the top, one bed, and sundry bits and pieces scattered around. My room was separated off from the next room by a large baize curtain hung on big wooden rings that slid back and forth with their *clack, clack, clack.* Behind the curtain was Anna's sofa bed. Outside my

bedroom window was a streetlamp, and as the window was only covered by lace curtains, the bedroom was always well lit. As I said, our house was right next to the railway, with trains passing all day and all night, but you got used to that. In fact, after nineteen years the rumble and rush of the passing trains was more of a lullaby than a noise.

When the bed had been made and all the night preparation attended to, I went back into the kitchen again. There was the little imp enthroned in a cane chair, swaddled in blankets, drinking a cup of hot cocoa. Bossy was sitting on her lap giving a fair imitation of Houdini trying to wriggle out of a straitjacket, and Patch was at her feet, beating time with his tail on the floor. The hiss of the gaslamp, the bright firelight, the little pools of water on the floor, all turned that little kitchen into a Christmas scene. The Welsh dresser, the shining pots and the black-leaded kitchen range, with its brass fire irons and guard, seemed to sparkle. In the midst of it all sat the little princess, clean and shining. This little thing had the most splendid, the most beautiful, copper-colored hair imaginable, and a face to match. No painted cherub on some church ceiling was this child, but a smiling, giggling, squirming, real live child, her face alight with some inner radiance, her eyes like two blue searchlights.

Earlier in the evening I had said yes to her question, "You love me, don't you?" because I was unable to say no. Now I was glad that I had been unable to say no, for the answer was yes. Yes. Yes. How could anyone fail to love this little thing?

Mum gave a bit of a grunt and her usual "Well, we had better get to bed or we won't be worth anything tomorrow." And so I picked up Anna and took her along to

11

her bed. The bedclothes were already pulled back and I put her down and made as if to tuck her up, but this was all wrong.

"Ain't you gonna say your prayers?" she asked.

"Well, yes," I replied, "when I get to bed."

"I want to say mine now with you," she said. So we both got down on our knees and she talked while I listened.

I've been to church many times, and heard many prayers, but none like this. I can't remember much about her prayer except that it started off with, "Dear Mister God, this is Anna talking," and she went on in such a familiar way of talking to Mister God that I had the creepy feeling that if I dared look behind me he would be standing there. I remember her saying, "Thank you for letting Fynn love me," and I remember being kissed good-night, but how I got to bed I don't know.

I lay in bed in some confusion wondering what had hit me. The trains rattled on their way, the fog swirled round the streetlamp. It may have been an hour that I had lain there, possibly two, when I heard the *clack, clack* of the curtain rings; and there she was standing at the end of my bed, quite visible in the lamplight. For a minute or two I lay there thinking that she was just wanting to reassure herself, when she moved around to the head of my bed.

I said, "Hi, Tich!"

"Can I get in?" she said in a whisper. She didn't wait for my "If you want to," but slid in beside me and buried her head in my neck and cried silently, her tears warm and wet on my chest. There was nothing to say, nothing to do but to put my arm around her. I didn't think I would sleep, but I did. I awoke to the sound of stifled giggles, Anna still beside me giggling like a fiend, and Carol, already dressed, standing there giggling, with a morning cup of tea in her hand. All this in less than twelve hours.

TWO During the next few weeks we tried to find out by a bit of cunning questioning where Anna lived. The gentle approach, the sideways approach, the sneaky approach—all proved to be useless. It seemed quite possible that she had just dropped out of heaven. I was ready to believe this to be true, but Stan, being much more practical than me, didn't agree at all. The only certain thing we knew was that she wasn't going to no bleeding cop shop. By this time I was sure that I had initiated this idea. After all, you don't find an orchid and then put it in the cellar. It wasn't that any of us had anything against the cops; far from it. In those days cops were more like official friends, even if they did clip you round the ear with a glove full of dried peas if they caught you up to any funny stuff. No, as I said, you can't lock a sunbeam in the dark. Besides, we all wanted her to stay.

By this time Anna was a firm favorite down our street. Whenever the kids played team games like four sticks, everyone wanted Anna on their side. She had a natural aptitude for all games: whip tops, skipping, cigarette cards. What she couldn't do with a hoop and a skimmer wasn't worth doing.

Our street, twenty houses big, was a regular United Nations; the only colors in kids we didn't have were green ones and blue ones, we had nearly every other color. Our street was a nice street. Nobody had any money, but in all the years I lived there, I can never remember anyone's front door being shut in the daytime, or, for that matter, for most of the night either. It was a nice street to live in and all the people were friendly, but after a few weeks of Anna the street and the people in it took on a butter- cup glow.

Even our boss-eyed cat, Bossy, mellowed. Bossy was a

fighting tabby with lace-edged ears who regarded all humans as inferiors, but under Anna's influence Bossy started to stay at home more often and very soon treated Anna as an equal. I could stand by the back door and yell myself silly for Bossy, but he wouldn't budge for me; but for Anna—well, that was a different thing. One call and he simply materialized with an idiot grin on his face.

Bossy was about twelve pounds of fighting fury, and I've got the scars to prove it. The cat's meat man used to leave the meat under the knocker, wrapped up in newspaper. Bossy used to lurk in the dark passageway, or under the stairs, waiting for someone to reach up for the cat's meat, at which moment he would launch himself like a fury, all teeth and claws, using whatever was available to get up to his meal. If a human leg or arm could be used to claw his way up to the meat, Bossy would use it. Anna tamed him in one day. She lectured him with an admonishing finger on the vice of gluttony and the virtues of patience and good manners. In the end, Bossy could make his meal last for about five minutes, with Anna feeding him bit by bit, instead of the usual thirty seconds. As for Patch the dog, he sat for hours practicing beating new rhythms with his tail.

In the back garden was an odd collection of rabbits, pigeons, fantail doves, frogs, and a couple of grass snakes. The back garden, or The Yard, as it was called, was for the East End a fairly sizable place. A bit of grass and a few flowers and a large tree some forty feet high. All in all, Anna had quite a lot to practice her magic on. But no one fell under her spell more completely or willingly than me. My work, which was in oils, was not more than five minutes' walk away from home, so I was always home for dinner at about twelve-thirty. Up to this time, the answer to Mum's question as to what time I would be home that night as I left for the afternoon's stint had been, Sometime before midnight. Now things were different. I was seen off by Anna from the top of the street, kissed wetly, promising to be back about six in the evening. Knocking-off time usually meant a few pints in the pub on the way home and a few games of darts with Cliff and George; but not now. When the hooter went, I was off home. I didn't run, exactly, but walked very briskly.

That walk home was a pleasure; every step was one step nearer. The road I had to travel curved to the left in a gentle arc, and I had to walk just more than half the distance before the top of our turning came into sight. And there she was. Come rain or shine, snow or icy wind, Anna was always there; not once did she miss this meeting, except—but that comes later. I doubt if ever lovers met more joyously. When she saw me coming round the bend of the road, she came to meet me.

Anna's ability to polish any situation was truly extraordinary. She had some uncanny knack of doing the right thing at the right time to get the most out of an occasion. I've always thought that children ran toward those they loved, but not Anna. When she saw me she started to walk toward me, not too slowly, but not too quickly. My first sight of her was too far away to distinguish her features; she might have been any other child, but she wasn't. Her beautiful copper hair stood out for miles; there was no mistaking her.

After her first few weeks with us she always wore a deep-green ribbon in her hair for this meeting. Looking back, I feel sure that the walk toward me was deliberate and calculated. She had grasped the meaning of these meetings and seen almost instantly just how much to dramatize them, how long to prolong them in order to wring out their total content. For me, this minute or two

of walk toward her had a rounded-off perfection; no more could be added to it, and nothing could be taken away without completely destroying it.

Whatever it was she projected across that intervening space was almost solid. Her bobbing hair, the twinkle in her eyes, that enormous and impudent grin, flicked like a high-voltage charge across the space that separated us. Sometimes she would, without any words, just touch my hand in greeting. Sometimes the last few steps transformed her; she let everything go with one gigantic explosion, and flung herself at me. So many times she would stop just in front of me and hold out her closed hands. I learned rapidly what to expect on these occasions. It meant that she had found something that had moved her. We would stop and inspect whatever the day's find was—perhaps a beetle, a caterpillar, or a stone. We would look silently, heads bowed over today's treasure. Her eyes were large deep pools of questions. How? Why? What? I'd meet her gaze and nod my head; this was enough, she'd nod in reply.

The first time this happened, my heart seemed to come off its hook. I struggled to hold on. I wanted to put my arms around her to comfort her. Happily, I managed to do the right thing. I guess some passing angel nudged me at the right moment. Unhappiness is to be comforted, and so perhaps too is fear, but these particular moments with Anna were moments of pure and undiluted wonder. These were her own and very private moments which she chose to share with me, and I was honored to share them with her. I could not comfort her, I would not have dared to trespass. All that I could do was to see as she saw, to be moved as she was moved. That kind of suffering, you must bear alone. As she said so simply, "It's for me and Mister God," and there's no answer to that.

The evening meal at home was more or less fixed. Mum, being the daughter of an Irish farmer, was given to making stews. A large black iron pot and an equally large black iron kettle were the two most used utensils in the kitchen. Often the only way one could distinguish the stew from the brew was that tea always came in large cups and stew was put on plates. Here the difference ended, for the brew often had as much solid matter in it as did the stew.

Mum was a great believer in the saying that nature grows cures for everything. There wasn't a weed or a flower or a leaf that wasn't a specific cure for some ailment or other. Even the outside shed was pressed into use for growing cobwebs. Some people have sacred cows or sacred cats—Mum had sacred spiders. I never quite understood the reasoning concerning spiders' webs, but all cuts and abrasions were plastered with spiders' webs. If spiders' webs were not available there were always cigarette papers under the clock in the kitchen. These were well licked and stuck over the cut. Our house was littered with bottles of juices, dried leaves, and bunches of this, that and the other, hanging from the ceiling. All ailments were treated the same way—rub it, lick it, or if you can't lick it, spit on it, or "Drink this, it'll do you good."

Whatever the value of these things, one thing was certain: nobody was ever ill. The only time the doctor entered our house was when something was suspected of being broken, and when Stan was born. No matter that the brew—or to give it its full title, "the darlin' brew"— and the stew looked the same; they tasted wonderful and meals were certainly man-sized.

Mum and Anna shared many likes and dislikes; perhaps the simplest and the most beautiful sharing was their attitude toward Mister God. Most people I knew used God as an excuse for their failure: "He should have done this," or "Why has God done this to me?" But with Mum and Anna difficulties and adversities were merely occasions for doing something. Ugliness was the chance to make beautiful. Sadness was the chance to make glad. Mister God was always available to them. A stranger would have been excused for believing that Mister God lived with us, but then Mum and Anna believed he did. Very rarely did any conversation exclude Mister God in some way or other.

After the evening meal was finished and all the bits and pieces put away, Anna and I would settle down to some activity, generally of her choosing. Fairy stories were dismissed as mere pretend stories; living was real and living was interesting, and by and large, fun. Reading the Bible wasn't a great success. She tended to regard it as a primer, strictly for the infants. The message of the Bible was simple and any half-wit could grasp it in thirty minutes flat! Religion was for doing things, not for reading about doing things. Once you had got the message there wasn't much point in going over and over the same old ground. Our local parson was taken aback when he asked her about God. The conversation went as follows:

"Do you believe in God?"

"Yes."

"Do you know what God is?"

"Yes."

"What is God then?"

"He's God!"

"Do you go to church?"

"No."

"Why not?"

"Because I know it all!"

"What do you know?"

"I know to love Mister God and to love people and cats and dogs and spiders and flowers and trees"—and the catalog went on—"with all of me."

Carol grinned at me, Stan made a face, and I hurriedly put a cigarette in my mouth and indulged in a bout of coughing. There's nothing much you can do in the face of that kind of accusation, for that's what it amounted to. ("Out of the mouths of babes . . .") Anna had bypassed all the nonessentials and distilled centuries of learning into one sentence: "And God said love me, love them, and love it, and don't forget to love yourself."

The whole business of adults going to church filled Anna with suspicion. The idea of collective worship went against her sense of private conversations with Mister God. As for going to church to meet Mister God, that was preposterous. After all, if Mister God wasn't everywhere, he wasn't anywhere. For her, churchgoing and "Mister God" talks had no necessary connection. For her, the whole thing was transparently simple. You went to church to get the message when you were very little. Once you had got it, you went out and did something about it. Keeping on going to church was because you hadn't got the message or didn't understand it or it was "just for swank."

After the evening meal I always read to Anna, books on all manner of subjects from poetry to astronomy. After a year of reading, she ended up with three favorite books. The first was a large picture book with nothing in it but photographs of snowflakes and frost patterns. The second book was Cruden's *Complete Concordance,* and the third, of all the strange books to choose, was Manning's *Geometry of Four Dimensions.* Each of these books had a catalytic effect on Anna. She devoured them utterly, and out of their digestion she produced her own philosophy.

One of her pleasures was my reading to her that part of the concordance given over to the meaning of proper names. Each name was read in strict alphabetical order
and the meaning given. After each name had been tasted and thought over she made her decision as to its rightness. Most times she shook her head sadly and disappointedly;

it wasn't good enough. Sometimes it was just right; the name, the person, the meaning, all fitted perfectly for her and, with a burst of excitement, she would bounce up and down on my lap and say, "Put it down, put it down." This meant writing the name in large block capitals on a slip of paper, which she would stare at with complete concentration for a minute or two and then place in one of her many boxes. A moment to compose herself, and, "Next one, please." So we would go on. Some names took all of fifteen minutes or more to decide one way or the other. The decision was made in complete silence. On the occasions when I moved to a more comfortable position, or started to speak, I was reprimanded with a tilt of the head, a full-blooded stare, and a small finger placed gently but firmly on my lips. I learned to wait patiently. It took us about four months to work through the section on proper names, moments of high excitement and moments of low disappointment, none of which I understood at that time. Later I was let into the secret.

Since our first meeting God had been given the title Mister God; the Holy Spirit, for some reason only known to her, was given the name Vehrak. I never heard her use the name Jesus. Whenever she referred to Jesus it was as Mister God's boy. One evening we were working our way through the J's and came eventually to Jesus. I had hardly got the name out before I was stopped by a "No!," a wagging finger, and "Next one, please." Who was I to argue? I pressed on. The next name on the list was Jether. I had to pronounce this three times, and then turning to me she said, "Read what it says." So I read:

"Jether, meaning he that excels or remains, or that examines, searches; or a line or string."

The effect of this was electric, catastrophic. With a blur of movement she had slipped off my lap, twisted about to face me and stood crouched with hands clenched, the whole of her being shaking with excitement. For one horrifying moment I thought she was ill or having a fit, but that wasn't the explanation. Whatever the explanation was it went deeper than anything I could understand. She was filled with joy. She kept saying, "It's true. I know it. It's true. It's true. I know it." With that she fled out into the yard. I made to go out after her but Mum put out a hand and held me back, saying, "Leave her alone, she's happy. She's got the eye." Half an hour passed before she returned. Without a word she climbed on to my lap, gave me one of her special grins and said, "Please write the name big for me tonight," and then went to sleep. She didn't even wake up when I put her to bed. It was months before the word epilepsy faded from my thoughts.

Mum always said that she pitied the girl that I married, for she would have to put up with my three mistresses—Mathematics, Physics, and Electrical Gadgetry. I would rather read and practice these subjects than eat or sleep. I never bought myself a wristwatch or a fountain pen, and very rarely did I buy new clothes, but I never went anywhere without a slide rule. This device fascinated Anna and soon she had to have a slip stick of her own. Having mastered the whole business of counting numbers, she was soon extracting roots with the aid of her slip stick before she could add two numbers together. Users of slip sticks soon fall into a stable method of using this device. It's held in the left hand, leaving the right hand free to hold the pencil; the "cursor" can be moved with the thumb and the sliding scale tapped against the workbench. One of my particular pleasures was seeing the copper-crowned, diminutive child doing her "workings out," as she called it. Looking down from a height of six foot or more and saying, "How you doing, Tich?" I'd see her head screw round and upward and watch one delicious wiggle start from her toes, pass up her body, to be tossed off the top of her head in a foam of silky copper thread, with a grin of absolute joy.

Some evenings were given over to piano playing. I play a fairly good honky-tonk piano, a bit of Mozart, a bit of Chopin, and a few pieces like "Anitra's Dance" just for good measure. On the top of the piano were several elec-

tronic devices. One device, the oscilloscope, held all the magic of a fairy wand for Anna. We'd sit in this room for hours on end playing single notes, watching the green spot on the 'scope do its glowing dance. The whole exercise of relating sounds that one heard with the ears to the visual shape of those sounds actively seen on the little tube's face was a source of never-ending delight.

What sounds we captured, Anna and I! A caterpillar chewing a leaf was like a hungry lion, a fly in a jam jar sounded like an airship, a match being struck sounded like an explosion. All these sounds and a thousand more were amplified and made available, both in sound form and visible form. Anna had found a brand-new world to explore. How much meaning it had for her I didn't know; perhaps it was only an elaborate plaything for her, but her squeals of delight were enough for me.

It was only sometime during the next summer that I began to realize that the concepts of frequency and wavelength were meaningful to her, that she did, in fact, know and understand what she was hearing and looking at. One summer afternoon all the kids were playing in the street when a large bumblebee appeared on the scene.

One of the kids said, "How many times does it flap its wings in a minute?"

"Must be millions," said another kid.

Anna dashed indoors humming a low-pitched hum. I was sitting on the doorstep. With a few quick prods at the piano she had identified the note, her hum, and the drone of the bee. Coming to the door again, she said, "Can I have your slip stick?" In a moment or two she shouted out, "A bee flaps its wings such-and-such times a second." Nobody believed her, but she was only a few counts out.

Every sound that could be captured was captured. Meals began to be punctuated with such remarks as, "Do you

know a mosquito flaps its wings so many times a second?"
or, "a fly, so many times a second?"

All these games led inevitably to making music. Each separate note had by this time been examined minutely, and a sound depended on how many times it wiggled per second. Soon she was making little melodies to which I added the harmonies. Little pieces of music entitled "Mummy," "Mr. Jether's Dance," and "Laughter" soon began to echo around the house. Anna had begun to compose. I suppose Anna only had one problem in her little life—the lack of hours per day. There was too much to do, too many exciting things to find out.

Another of Anna's magic carpets was the microscope. It revealed a little world made big. A world of intricate shape and pattern, a world of creatures too small to see with the naked eye; even the very dirt itself was wonderful.

Before all this adventuring into these hidden worlds, Mister God had been Anna's friend and companion, but now, well this was going a bit too far. If Mister God had done all this, he was something larger than Anna had bargained for. It needed a bit of thinking about. For the next few weeks, activity slowed down; she still played with the other children in the street; she was still as sweet and exciting as ever; but she became more inward-looking, more inclined to sit alone, high in the tree in the yard, with only Bossy as her companion. Whichever way she looked there seemed to be more and more of everything.

During these few weeks Anna slowly took stock of all she knew, walking about gently touching things as if looking for some clue that she had missed. She didn't talk much in this period. In reply to questions, she answered as simply as she could, apologizing for her absence by the gentlest of smiles, saying without words, "I'm sorry about all this. I'll be back as soon as I've sorted this little puzzle out." Finally the whole thing came to a head.

She turned to me. "Can I come to bed with you to-night?" she asked.

I nodded.

"Now," she replied.

She hopped off my lap, took my hand, and pulled me to the door. I went.

I haven't told you Anna's way of solving problems, have I? If Anna was confronted with a situation that didn't come out easily, there was only one thing to do—take your clothes off. So there we were in bed, the street-lamp lighting up the room, her head cupped in her hands, and both elbows firmly planted on my chest. I waited. She chose to remain like that for about ten minutes, getting her argument in its proper order, and then she launched forth.

"Mister God made everything, didn't he?"

There was no point in saying that I didn't really know. I said "Yes."

"Even the dirt and the stars and the animals and the people and the trees and everything, and the pollywogs?" The pollywogs were those little creatures that we had seen under the microscope.

I said, "Yes, he made everything."

She nodded her agreement. "Does Mister God love us truly?"

"Sure thing," I said. "Mister God loves everything."

"Oh," she said. "Well then, why does he let things get hurt and dead?" Her voice sounded as if she felt she had betrayed a sacred trust, but the question had been thought and it had to be spoken.

26

"I don't know," I replied. "There're a great many things about Mister God that we don't know about."

"Well then," she continued, "if we don't know many things about Mister God, how do we know he loves us?"

I could see that this was going to be one of those times, but thank goodness she didn't expect an answer to her question, for she hurried on: "Them pollywogs, I could love them till I bust, but they wouldn't know, would they? I'm million times bigger than they are and Mister God is million times bigger than me, so how do I know what Mister God does?"

She was silent for a little while. Later I thought that at this moment she was taking her last look at babyhood. Then she went on.

"Fynn, Mister God doesn't love us." She hesitated. "He doesn't really, you know, only people can love. I love Bossy, but Bossy don't love me. I love the pollywogs, but they don't love me. I love you, Fynn, and you love me, don't you?"

I tightened my arm about her.

"You love me because you are people. I love Mister God truly, but he don't love me."

It sounded to me like a death knell. "Damn and blast," I thought. "Why does this have to happen to people? Now she's lost everything." But I was wrong. She had got both feet planted firmly on the next stepping-stone.

"No," she went on, "no, he don't love me, not like you do, it's different, it's millions of times bigger."

I must have made some movement or noise, for she levered herself upright and sat on her haunches and giggled. Then she launched herself at me and undid my little pang of hurt, cut out the useless spark of jealousy with the delicate sureness of a surgeon.

"Fynn, you can love better than any people that ever was, and so can I, can't I? But Mister God is different. You see, Fynn, people can only love outside and can only kiss outside, but Mister God can love you right inside, and Mister God can kiss you right inside, so it's different. Mister God ain't like us; we are a little bit like Mister God, but not much yet."

It seemed to me to reduce itself to the fact that we were like God because of some similarities, but God was not like us because of our difference. Her inner fires had refined her ideas, and like some alchemist she had turned lead into gold. Gone were all the human definitions of God, like Goodness, Mercy, Love, and Justice, for these were merely props to describe the indescribable.

"You see, Fynn, Mister God is different from us because he can finish things and we can't. I can't finish loving you because I shall be dead millions of years before I can finish, but Mister God can finish loving you, and so it's not the same kind of love, is it? Even Mister Jether's love is not the same as Mister God's because he only came here to make us remember."

The first salvo was enough for me; it all needed a bit of thinking about, but I wasn't going to be spared the rest of her artillery.

"Fynn, why do people have fights and wars and things?"

I explained to the best of my ability.

"Fynn, what is the word for when you see it in a different way?"

After a minute or two scrabbling about, the precise phrase she wanted was dredged out of me, the phrase, *point of view*.

"Fynn, that's the difference. You see, everybody has got a point of view, but Mister God hasn't. Mister God has only points *to* view."

At this moment my one desire was to get up and go for a long, long walk. What was this child up to? What had she done? In the first place, God could finish things off, I couldn't. I'll accept that, but what did it mean? It seemed to me that she had taken the whole idea of God outside the limitation of time and placed him firmly in the realm of eternity.

What about this difference between *a point of view* and *points to view?* This stumped me, but a little further questioning cleared up the mystery. *Points to view* was a clumsy term. She meant *viewing points.* The second salvo had been fired. Humanity in general had an infinite number of points of view, whereas Mister God had an infinite number of viewing points. When I put it to her this way and asked her if that was what she meant, she nodded her agreement and then waited to see if I enjoyed the taste. Let me see now. Humanity has an infinite number of points of view. God has an infinite number of viewing points. That means that—God is everywhere. I jumped.

Anna burst into peals of laughter. "You see," she said, "you see?" I did, too.

"There's another way that Mister God is different." We obviously hadn't finished yet. "Mister God can know things and people from the inside, too. We only know them from the outside, don't we? So you see, Fynn, people can't talk about Mister God from the outside; you can only talk about Mister God from the inside of him."

Another fifteen minutes or so were spent in polishing up these arguments and then, with an "Isn't it lovely?" she kissed me and tucked herself under my arm, ready for sleep.

About ten minutes later: "Fynn?"

"Yes?"

"Fynn, you know that book about four dimensions?"

"Yes, what about it?"

"I know where number four is; it goes inside me."

I'd had enough for that night, and said with all the firmness and authority I could muster, "Go to sleep now. That's enough talking for tonight. Go to sleep or I'll paddle your bottom."

She made a little screech, looked at me, and grinned and squirmed in closer to me. "You wouldn't!" she said sleepily.

Anna's first summer with us was days of adventures and visits. We visited Southend-on-Sea, Kew Gardens, the Kensington Museum, and a thousand other places, most times alone, but sometimes with a gang of other kids. Our first excursion outside the East End was "up the other end." For anyone not familiar with that term, it simply means west of Aldgate pump.

On this occasion she was dressed in a tartan skirt with shirtblouse, a black tammy, black shoes with large shiny buckles, and tartan socks. The skirt was tightly pleated so that a twirl produced a parachute-like effect. Anna walked like a pro, jumped like Bambi, flew like a bird, and balanced like a daring tightrope walker on the curbs. Anna copied her walk from Millie, who was a pro—head held high, the slight sway of body making her skirts swing, a smile on her face, a twinkle in her eye—and you were defenseless. People looked and people smiled. Anna was a burst of sunlight after weeks of gloom. Of course people smiled, they couldn't help it. Anna was completely aware of these glances from passersby, occasionally turning her head to look at me with a big, big grin of pleasure. Danny said she never walked, she made a royal progress. Her progress was halted from time to time by her subjects: stray pussies, dogs, pigeons, and horses, to say nothing of postmen, milkmen, bus conductors, and policemen.

As we walked west of Aldgate pump the buildings got

grander and bigger and Anna's mouth opened further and further. She walked round and round in small circles, she walked backward, sideways, and every way. Finally she stopped in bewilderment, tugged at my sleeve, and asked, "Does kings and queens live in them and are they all palaces?"

She didn't find the Bank of England very impressive, nor for that matter, St. Paul's; the pigeons won hands down. After a little talk we decided to go into the service. She was very uncomfortable, fidgeting about the whole while. As soon as the service was over we hurried outside and made straight for the pigeons. She sat on the pavement and fed them with great pleasure. I stood a few paces off and just watched her. Her eyes flicked from place to place: at the doors of the cathedral, the passersby, the traffic, and the pigeons. Occasionally she tossed her head in disapproval of something. I looked about me to see what it was that affected her so much. There was nothing that I could see which would account for her mood.

After some months I could now read her distress signal accurately. That sharp little toss of the head wasn't a good sign. To me, it always looked as if she was trying to dislodge some unpleasant thought in the same way that one might shake a money box to get the coins out.

I went over to her and stood waiting. Most times just being near her was all the trigger she needed. The move toward her wasn't in order to give her counsel. Long ago I had given that up. Her reply to the question, "What's up, Tich?" was invariably the same: "I can get it, I think." On those occasions when she couldn't get the answers, then and only then would she ask questions. No, my reason for moving over to her was simply that my ears were at the ready if she needed them. She didn't, and that was a very bad sign.

From St. Paul's we moved off toward Hyde Park. After all these months I was beginning to be rather proud of the fact that more and more I was learning to think along with Anna. I was beginning to understand the way she thought and the way she said things. This particular afternoon I had forgotten, no, not forgotten, hadn't realized one simple fact. It was this: up to now Anna's visual horizon had been one of houses, factories, cranes, and a toppling inward of structure. Suddenly there were the open, and to her, the *very* open spaces of the park. I wasn't ready for her reaction. She took one look, buried her face in my stomach, grabbed me with both hands, and howled. I picked her up and she clung to me like a limpet, arms tight around my neck, and legs around my waist, sobbing into my neck. I made all the appropriate noises, but this didn't help much.

After a few minutes she took a sneaky look over her shoulder and stopped crying.

I said, "Want to go home, Tich?" and she shook her head.

"You can put me down now," she said.

I think I had expected her to give one whoop and gallop off across the grass. A couple of hearty sniffs and a moment or two to gain her composure, and we started off to explore the park, but she held on to my hand very tightly. Like any other child, Anna had her fears, but unlike most children, she recognized them. And with this recognition came the realization that she could go on in spite of them.

How can any adult know the exact weight of that fright? Does it mean that the child is timid, alarmed, anxious, petrified, or frozen stiff with terror? Is a ten-headed monster more frightening than an idea? If she hadn't exactly mastered her fear, whatever it was, she had got it well under control. By now she was prepared to let go of my hand, to make a little sortie after something that interested her, always looking back to make sure I was there. So I stopped in my tracks and waited for her. She was still a little bit scared and she knew that I was aware that she was scared too. The fact that I stopped whenever she let go of my hand brought forth a grateful little smile of acknowledgement.

My mind flipped back to the time when I was her age. My mother and father had taken me to Southend-on-Sea. The sight of the sea and the press of all those people was like being hit by a bus. I had been holding my father's hand when I first had a sight of the sea, and then, suddenly, I was holding a stranger's hand. I can't remember very much except that then and there the world came to an end. So I did have some inkling of her fears, whatever they were.

Her little explorations were slowly bringing things back to normal. She'd return with her usual treasures, different-shaped leaves, stone, bits of twigs, etc. Her enthusiasm could not be restrained any longer.

Suddenly I heard the gruff shout of a park keeper. I turned, and there she was, kneeling in front of a flower bed. I had forgotten to tell her to keep off the grass. Anna would not have given way to Lucifer himself and certainly not to a park keeper. Having negotiated one catastrophe, I didn't want to face another. I ran and scooped her into my arms and stood her down on the pathway.

"He," she said indignantly, pointing an accusing finger, "told me to get off the grass."

"Yes," I replied, "you're not supposed to be on this bit of grass."

"But it's the best bit," she said.

"See those words." I pointed to the notice. "They say KEEP OFF THE GRASS."

She studied the notice with great concentration as I spelled out the words for her.

Later that afternoon, while we were sitting on the grass eating chocolate, she said, "Them words."

"What words?" I asked.

"Them words that say to keep off the grass—them words are like that church we went to this morning."

Then it all became apparent. Like the flower beds, the church service had been to Anna nothing less than a notice saying KEEP OFF THE GRASS. She couldn't get at the best bits. To be inside a church—not at a church service, but simply to be inside—was for Anna like visiting a very, very special friend, and visiting a very special friend is a happy occasion; and that, surely, is a good enough reason to dance. Inside a church Anna danced; it was the best bit. Church services, therefore, like the Keep Off the Grass notices, did not allow her to have the best bit. I smiled as I pictured the kind of service that Anna would have liked. I'm not so sure that Mister God wouldn't have preferred it too!

Having started to unburden herself, she pressed on with, "You know when I cried?"

I grunted my attention.

"It didn't half make me small, so small I nearly got lost." This, in a small and far-off voice; and then zooming back from an infinity of space and landing with a thump on my chest, she went on triumphantly, "But I didn't, did I?"

It was sometime toward the end of this first summer that she made two most startling discoveries. The first was seeds—that things grew from seeds, that all this beauty, these flowers, these trees, this lovely grass, came from seeds, and moreover that you could actually hold these seeds in your hands. The second major discovery

34

was writing—that books and writing in general had a much more exciting aspect to them than merely being the machinery for telling stories. She saw writing as a portable memory, as a means of exchanging information.

These two discoveries started off a frenzy of activity. Anna's thought processes and bodily activity were such that on occasions it was very nearly possible actually to see the pictures in her mind.

The first day she held flower seeds in her hand was such a time. There was no need for words; her actions and thoughts spoke for themselves. There she was in front of some wild flowers, kneeling down with a sprinkling of seeds in her hands. Her eyes located her thoughts; she looked at the seeds and her brow furrowed. She looked over her shoulder into the distance and her eyes popped in amazement, back to the seeds, back over her shoulder. Finally she stood up, looked outward—where to, I do not know—and slowly turned a full circle. By the time she faced me, her inner lamps had been turned full on.

I didn't have to be told what was going on in her head; it was plain to see. The sharp needle of her thoughts had sewn together this flower-filled scene that we now occupied with the bare patches of land in the East End. Of course seeds could be transported from one place to another, so why not do it? She looked at me with large question marks in her eyes, and without a word I gave her my clean pocket handkerchief. She spread this on the ground, and with infinite care shook the seed pods. The white handkerchief was soon covered with the dark grains of the seeds.

This activity of collecting seeds was one that I saw thousands of times; never once was she violent with any seed pod, and on each and every occasion came the moment of decision: "Have I taken too many?" "Are there enough left?" Sometimes the decision could only be made after a careful inspection of the seed pods. If she decided she had taken too many she would then proceed to portion out those seeds she had collected, sprinkling very carefully some portion back on the land again. Mister God went up about ten points in her estimation with regard to these seeds as she said, "Ain't Mister God wonderful!"

Anna was not only deeply in love with Mister God; she was proud of him. Anna's pride in Mister God grew and grew to such dimensions that in some idiot moment I wondered if Mister God ever went pink with pleasure. Whatever feelings people have had about Mister God over the many centuries, I'm very sure of one thing—nobody has ever liked Mister God more than Anna.

These excursions into the realm of seeds meant that a large supply of envelopes was carried with us and a large pouch was fixed around Anna's waist. The pouch was fixed onto a rather splendid beaded belt made for her by Millie. Millie was one of the dozen or so pros who had a house at the top of the street. Millie and Jackie were, according to Anna, the two most beautiful young ladies in the whole world. Between this young prostitute and Anna, there developed a mutual admiration society. Just in passing, Millie had the rich name of the Venus de Mile End.

Anna's other major discovery of that summer grew into a very complex activity, for our house suddenly blossomed with little blue notebooks and slips of paper. When confronted with something new, Anna would accost the nearest passerby, and hold out notebook and pencil, with a "Please write that down big, please."

THREE

This request to "write it down big" often produced a somewhat startled reaction. Anna's presentation on these occasions was like a stick of dynamite with a very, very short fuse, and it frightened some people. To be confronted by a redheaded, five-year-old kid, to have a notebook and pencil thrust into your hand, and to be requested to write it down big was for a lot of people unnerving, to say the least. People shied away with that kind of look; they replied with "Buzz off, kid," "Don't bother me, kid," but Anna expected this sort of thing and pressed on regardless. Anna's ship of discovery was now fully under way. True, it might leak a bit here and there, and the seas of knowledge could become a little rough at times, but there was no turning back. There were things to be discovered and Anna meant to discover them.

Many and many an evening I would be sitting on the steps smoking a cigarette and watching her asking people to write it down big, enjoying her search for knowledge. One particular evening, after a row of refusals on the part of passersby, Anna began to sag. I reckoned it was about time to dish out a few words of comfort. I levered myself off the steps and crossed the road to her.

She pointed to a broken-off stump of an iron railing. "I want somebody to write about that, but they don't see it."

"Perhaps they are too busy," I suggested.

"No it ain't. They don't see it. They don't know what I mean."

This last reply was uttered with a kind of deep and inward sadness; it was a sentence that I was to hear more and more. "They don't see it. They don't see it."

I had read the disappointment on her face and knew what to do—or thought I knew. This was the kind of situation that I figured I could handle. I picked her up and held her close to me.

"Don't be too disappointed, Tich."

"Not disappointed. Sad."

"Never mind," I said, "I'll write it down big for you."

She wriggled herself out of my arms and stood on the pavement, her hands fiddling with the notebook and pencil, head bowed and with tears on her cheeks. My mind raced around in circles. A number of methods of approach jostled each other. Just as I was about to "put it all right again" that passing angel fetched me a crack on the skull again. So I remained silent and waited. She stood there in utter dejection. I knew for certain, I told myself, knew for certain that she wanted to run to my arms, knew that she wanted comforting, but she just stood there wrestling inwardly. Trams clanked on their way, people shopped, barrow boys shouted their wares, and there we stood, me fighting against picking her up and she staring at some new picture painted on her mind.

At last she looked up and her eyes met mine. It suddenly got cold, and I wanted to hit somebody. I knew this look, I had seen it before in other people and it had happened to me more than once. Like some monstrous iceberg appearing out of the fog, the word formed, welling up from deep inside me, haloed with tears but nonetheless clear to see. Anna was mourning. All the doors of her eyes and heart stood wide open and that lonely cell of her inmost being stood plain to see.

"I don't want you to write nuffink." She tried out a smile but it didn't work too well, and with a sniff she continued, "I know what I see and I know what you see, but some people don't see nuffink and—and—." She threw herself into my arms and sobbed.

On that evening in a street in East London I stood with a child in my arms and looked into that lonely cell of humanity. No book learning, no lecture has shown me more than those few moments. Lonely the cell may be, but dark, never. It wasn't dark behind those tear-filled eyes, but a blaze of light. And God made man in his own image, not in shape, not in intelligence, not in eyes or ears, not in hands or feet, but in this total inwardness. In here was the image of God. It isn't the devil in humanity that makes man a lonely creature, it's his God-likeness. It's the fullness of the Good that can't get out or can't find its proper "other place" that makes for loneliness.

Anna's misery was for others. They just could not see the beauty of that broken iron stump, the colors, the crystalline shapes; they could not see the possibilities there. Anna wanted them to join with her in this exciting new world, but they could not imagine themselves to be so small that this jagged fracture could become a world of iron mountains, of iron plains with crystal trees. It was a new world to explore, a world of the imagination, a world where few people would or could follow her. In this broken-off stump was a whole new realm of possibilities to be explored and to be enjoyed.

Mister God most certainly enjoyed it, but then Mister God didn't at all mind making himself small. People thought that Mister God was very big, and that's where they made a big mistake. Obviously Mister God could be any size he wanted to be. "If he couldn't be little, how could he know what it's like to be a ladybird?" Indeed, how could he? So, like Alice in Wonderland, Anna ate of the cake of imagination and altered her size to fit the occasion. After all, Mister God did not have only one point of view but an infinity of viewing points, and the whole purpose of living was to be like Mister God. So far as Anna was concerned, being good, being generous, being kind, praying, and all that kind of stuff had very little to do with Mister God. They were, in the jargon of today, merely "spin-offs." This sort of thing was just "playing it safe," and Anna was going to have none of it. No! Religion was all about *being* like Mister God and it was here that things could get a little tough. The instructions weren't to be good and kind and loving, etc., and it therefore followed that you would be more like Mister God. No! The whole point of being alive was to *be* like Mister God and then you couldn't help but be good and kind and loving, could you?

"If you get like Mister God, you don't know you are, do you?"

"Are what?" I questioned.

"Good and kind and loving."

This last comment was delivered in her throw-away tone of voice as if it were insignificant and irrelevant. I knew this one of old. Either you had to pretend it hadn't happened, or start asking questions. A moment or two of hesitation on my part as I watched the grin spread from her toes and explode in one short sharp hoot of mirth, and I realized that she had sprung the trap. She had something to say and had forced me into asking the question. If I hadn't done it then I would have had to sooner or later, so . . .

"OK, Tich. What's all this goodness and kindness and loving lark then?"

"Well," and the tone of her voice slid down the roller

coaster of excitement, shot up the other side, and took off. "Well, if you think you are, you ain't."

From my position at the bottom of this particular class I asked, "How come?"

I thought I had got the drift of this conversation and reckoned I was waiting for her about two steps ahead. She had signalled a right turn and I was waiting for her, but suddenly she took a left-handed U-turn and sped back against the oncoming arguments. Thrown off balance by this sudden switch, I could do no more than walk back to where she was waiting.

"Right. Give!" I said.

"You don't expect Mister God *knows* he is good and kind and loving, do you?"

I don't suppose I had ever given this a moment's thought, but put like that there was only one answer to give, even though I wasn't convinced of the truth of it.

"I guess not," I replied, with some hesitation.

The question Why? got stuck somewhere between my brainbox and my vocal chords. I should have known that the whole of this conversation was leading to some conclusion, some idea, some statement that satisfied her completely. She gathered herself, holding her excitement in check.

Suddenly, with an explosive gasp, she said, "Mister God don't know he is good and kind and loving. Mister God is—is—empty."

Now I'll accept that the stone that bruises my toe isn't really there. I don't mind entertaining the idea that everything is an illusion, but that Mister God is empty simply goes against the grain. It stands to reason that Mister God is full! Full of knowing, full of love, full of compassion—you name it, and he is full of it. Why God is like some—some gigantic Christmas stocking full of good presents, inexhaustible, showering untold and unnumbered presents upon his children. Damnation, of course he's full! That's what I was taught and that's how it was —or was it?

I got no more from Anna that day or for several days after. I stewed in my own juice. The idea that Mister God was empty milled around in my brain. Of course it was ridiculous, but it just stuck there. As a picture formed in my mind, I got more and more embarrassed and more and more ashamed. I hadn't seen this picture with such clarity before, but there he was, Mister God all dressed up in a dress suit, top hat, and a wand, producing rabbits out of a hat. You put up your hand and asked for a motorcar, a thousand pounds, or what you will, and Mister God waved his magic wand and out it all came. In the end I saw my picture of Mister God—a kindly, benevolent, and bewhiskered *magician*.

A few days later, after a lot of wondering how came this idea that Mister God was quite empty, I asked the question that had puzzled me for days.

"Tich! What's with this Mister God being empty stuff?"

She turned to me eagerly. I distinctly got the impression that she had waited for this question for days but could do nothing until I had seen my picture of Mister God, the great magician.

"When the world went all red through the bit a glass, and the color from the flower."

I remembered that, all right. We had talked about transmitted light and reflected light: that light took on the color of the glass through which it was transmitted, that the color of the yellow flower was due to reflected light. We had seen the colors of the spectrum with the aid of a prism, we had looked at Newton's colored spinning disc and had mixed all the colors of the spectrum back to white again. I had explained that the yellow flower absorbed all the colors of the spectrum, with the exception of yellow, which was reflected back to the viewer. Anna had digested this bit of information for a while and then had come back with: "Oh! Yellow is the bit it *don't* want!" and after a little pause, "So its real color is all the bits it *do* want."

I couldn't argue with this since I couldn't be sure what the heck a flower would want anyway.

All these bits of information had been taken in, mixed with various bits of colored glass, shaken well, and worked into her particular framework. It seemed that each and every individual was issued at birth with various bits of glass labeled, GOOD, BAD, NASTY, etc., etc. People got into the habit of slipping these bits of glass over their inward eye and seeing things according to the color and label of the glass. This we did, I was given to understand, in order to justify our inner convictions.

Now, Mister God was a bit different from a flower. A flower that didn't want the yellow light was called yellow by us because that is what we saw. You couldn't say the same thing about Mister God. Mister God wanted everything, so he didn't reflect anything back! Now if Mister God didn't reflect anything back, we couldn't possibly see him, could we? So as far as we are concerned, so far as we were able to understand what Mister God was, we simply had to admit that Mister God was quite empty. Not empty because there was truly nothing there, but empty because he accepted everything, because he wanted everything and did not reflect anything back! Of course you could cheat if you wanted to; you could wear your bit of colored glass marked MISTER GOD IS LOVING or the bit marked MISTER GOD IS KIND, but then, of course, you would miss the whole nature of Mister God. Just imagine what kind of an "object" Mister God must be if he accepts everything, if he reflects absolutely nothing back. This, said Anna, is being a *real God*. This is what we were being asked to do, throw away our pieces of colored glass and see clearly. The fact that Old Nick was busy turning them out by the million made things a bit difficult at times, but that was the way things were.

"Sometimes," said Anna, "growed-ups make kids have bits a glass."

"Why would they want to do that?" I asked.

"So they can make the kids do something they want them to."

"You mean frighten them?"

"Yes. To do something."

"Like God will punish you if you don't eat up your prunes?"

"Yes, like that. But Mister God don't care if you don't like prunes, do he?"

"I guess not."

"If he did punish you for that he would be a big bully, and he ain't."

Most people are lucky if they ever discover the world in which they live. Anna had discovered unnumbered worlds through her "bits a colored glass," optical filters, mirrors, and garden witch-balls. The only problems with these many worlds was that more often than not you soon ran out of words to describe what you saw. I can't ever remember Anna using the words *noun* or *verb*, and certainly she couldn't tell an adjective from a ham sandwich, but she very soon came to the conclusion that the most hazardous aspect of writing or talking was the use of descriptive words. She'd go along with the statement that a rose is a rose is a rose—well almost go along with it—but that red is red is red was something else again.

The problem with words got further complicated by Mrs. Sussums. Mrs. Sussums had met us in the street. Mrs. Sussums was, in fact, Aunt Dolly, an aunt by marriage, and Aunt Dolly had one great passion in her life. This was eating nut toffee. She ate it in enormous quantities, continuously; and consequently her face always looked somewhat deformed by the presence of a large lump of toffee. If one was critical of Aunt Dolly it was because she always insisted on kissing everybody, not once but many times. Taken separately, the toffee-eating and the kissing were manageable, but together—well, it could become a bit dangerous.

We didn't manage to dodge the kissing. We were instructed to "open our mouths," and something about the size of a slab of toffee was popped in. That is to say about half of it went inside; the rest had to stay outside and wait.

After years of toffee-eating, Aunt Dolly's face muscles had developed quite remarkable strength, which enabled her to talk in spite of the glue strength of the toffee. Holding Anna at arm's length, she said, "My, isn't she big!"

I shifted gear with the toffee and managed, "Ga gig, guite gig!"

Anna came out with something that sounded like, "Gok gum gockle," which I hoped was translatable.

Aunt Dolly bade us good-bye and went on her way. We sat on a wall and coaxed the toffee into a manageable size and position.

Before Aunt Dolly's arrival we had been walking

along the street, or rather, we had been progressing along the street in a somewhat crazy way. You see, we had invented a game which could make a couple of hundred yards' walk take about two hours. Somebody was the "caller" and the other person was the "doer." The idea was that the caller would name some object on the ground—say a matchstick—and the doer would stand upon it. The caller would then name some other object and the doer would have to reach this other object in one step or leap. Hence, the somewhat erratic progress; there was no guarantee what direction the doer would take. We restarted our game. We had gone a matter of twenty yards or so in as many minutes when Anna stopped.

"Fynn, we both be doers and I'll be caller too."

So off we set, Anna doing the calling and we both, the doing, only this time it was different. No giggling this time, no squeaks of "I've found one. I've found a tram ticket." This time it was altogether too earnest. Anna muttered to herself at every step, "little step-hop, little step-hop, big step-hop," and then stopped. Looking back over the last step, she turned her head to me and said, "Was that a big step?"

"Not very."

"It was for me."

"That's because you're just a tich," I grinned.

"Auntie Dolly said I was big."

"She probably meant you were big for your age," I replied.

As an explanation, this didn't satisfy her one bit. The game stopped dead. She turned towards me, hands on hips. I could see her thinking apparatus itching with the woolliness of words.

46

"It don't mean nuffink," she said, like a judge putting on the black cap.

"Well it does," I tried to explain. "It means compared to a lot of little girls of five-and-a-bit years of age, you are bigger than most."

"Well then, if them girls was ten I would be littler, wouldn't I?"

"Could be."

"If I was the only one I wouldn't be littler or bigger, would I? I'd just be me, wouldn't I?"

I nodded my agreement. I could feel the tide coming in again, I could feel her working up to something, so I tried one last sentence before I was submerged.

"Look, Tich, you don't use words like *bigger* or *lovelier* or *smaller* or *sweeter* unless you've got some other thing to compare them with."

"Then you can't then, not always." There was a note of confidence in her voice.

"Can't what?" I asked.

"Can't compare, 'cos," and Anna fired her salvo of big guns, " 'cos Mister God. There ain't two Mister Gods so you can't compare."

"People don't compare Mister God with themselves."

"I know," she giggled at my efforts to defend myself.

"So what are you getting all fuzzed up about then?"

" 'Cos, 'cos they compare themselves with Mister God."

"Same difference," I replied.

"Ain't."

I reckoned I had won this particular exchange since my questions had forced her into a wrong move. After all, she had agreed that people didn't compare Mister God with themselves, so it followed that they didn't compare themselves with Mister God, and I told her so. Preparing to move to the top of the class on this particular exchange, I launched my unsinkable man-o'-war with, "You said people *did* compare. You should have said that people *didn't* compare."

Anna looked at me. I hurriedly manned the guns. I knew that I was right but I was going to be prepared, just in case. Anna looked, and my unsinkable man-o'-war just disappeared. I can remember feeling bad that she had handcuffed herself with her own arguments, feeling bad that it had been to some extent my fault and feeling bad that I had enjoyed winning this exchange. She moved close to me and put her arms around me and buried her head in the base of my chest. I thought how tired she must be with all this thinking, how disappointed she must feel because she "hadn't got it." All the doors of my storehouse of comfort and love opened wide and I hugged her. She gave a little wriggle to signify that she understood.

"Fynn," she said quietly, "compare two with three."

"One less," I murmured in a fug of contentment.

"Um. Now compare three with two."

"One more."

"That's right, one less is the same as one more."

"Uh-huh," I grunted, "one less is the same as— *Hey!*"

Suddenly she was ten yards away, doubled up with mirth and hooting like a banshee.

"It isn't the same," I yelled after her.

"It is, too," she bellowed.

I chased her home through the stalls and barrows of the market street. I didn't catch her. Being so much smaller than me, she got through places that I couldn't squeeze through physically, or for that matter, mentally, either.

That evening, sitting on the railway wall watching the trains go by, I said, "I suppose that was a bit of your famous glass?"

She made a noise that I took to be yes. After a little

pause I continued with, "How many bits of glass are you lumbered with?"

"I got millions, but they're all for fun."

"What about the bits you can't get rid of?" I went on.

"I have."

"Have what?"

"Got rid of them."

The complete matter-of-fact tone with which she uttered this last statement robbed me of my next sentence. Buzzing around in my brainbox were such ought-to-be-said sentences as Pride goes before a fall and The devil rides the backs of those who are certain. I had this nice adult feeling that I *ought* to take her down a peg or two; she *ought* not to make such remarks. After all, the only reason such corrective remarks were jostling around in my head was that it was good for her. I wanted to say these things for her benefit. It was my duty to say such things, and this gave me a nice warm virtuous and comforting feeling. The angel flew on his way without fetching me the usual crack on the skull so I knew that I was safe. I'd got the green light, so I could proceed. My stew of platitudes, proverbs, and general good advice had got to the "fast-rolling boil stage," so I opened my mouth to deliver all this wisdom. Trouble was, it didn't come out. Instead I asked, "You reckon you know more than Reverend Castle?"

"Nope."

"He got bits of glass?"

"Yes."

"How come you haven't got bits of glass?"

The shunting engine on the railway line marshalled its charges with a blast of steam and a whoop: a couple of toots of warning, a rheumatic squeal of its joints, and it shoved. The trucks woke up and passed the message down the line: *Ting-bong-tibang-bing-bong-bang-ti-clank.* It reached the end of the line and then back to the engine came the message, "OK, we're all awake, quit that blasted whistling." I grinned as I thought that the tank engine and Anna might be related in some way. They both had the same sort of technique. The engine shoved the trucks and Anna shoved me into asking the kind of questions she wanted to answer.

She didn't need to think about the answer to my question How come you haven't got bits of glass? She'd had it ready for a long time, simply waiting for the right moment to deliver it. She didn't make a fuss about delivering it, either: "Oh, 'cos I ain't frightened." Now, that's probably the most missable sentence that can be uttered. Missable because that's what it's all about. Missable because it is too damned expensive. Missable because the price of not being frightened is *trust.* And what a word *that* is! Define it how you like, and I'll bet you'll miss the main point! It's more than confidence, more than security; it doesn't belong to ignorance, or for that matter, to knowledge either. It is simply the ability to move out of the "I'm the center of all things" and to let something or someone take over. And as for Anna, she had simply moved out and let Mister God move in. I'd known about this for a long time.

I like mathematics. I see it as the most beautiful, most exciting, most poetic, and the most sublime of all activities. I have, and have had for many years, a little plaything, a toy, something I like to consider and something which sparks off ideas in me. It is simply two circles of heavy copper wire linked together like two links of a chain. I play with this so often that at times I am quite unaware that I have it in my hands. On one occa-

sion I was holding it so that the circles stood at right angles to each other.

Anna pointed to one of the circles and said, "I know what that is—that's me. And that's Mister God," she said, pointing to the other. "Mister God goes right through my middle and I go right through Mister God's middle."

And that's how it was. Anna had grasped that her proper place was in God's middle and that God's proper place was in her middle. That might be a little difficult to come upon for the first time, but the taste of it gets nicer and nicer; and of course Anna's " 'Cos I ain't frightened" was completely without blemish. This was her structure, her satisfactory picture of how things were, and I envied her.

It wasn't very often that Anna was taken completely off her guard. But on one particular occasion I actually saw a spoonful of raisin pudding and custard arrested in midair. It happened like this. Ma B. had a pudding shop. Ma B. was one of nature's miracles; she was taller when she was lying down than when she was standing up. I suppose it was because she ate her own puddings.

Ma B. had reduced the English language to real basic stuff. She had the use of two sentences: "What's yours, ducks?" and "Fancy that!" What Ma B. lacked in the way of the melody of the language, she made up for by orchestration. "Fancy that!" could be orchestrated to signify surprise, indignation, horror, or any feeling or mixture of feelings appropriate to the moment. When Ma B. wheezed out, "What's yours, ducks?" the request for "two of meat pud and two of peas pud" was often followed by such juicy bits as, "What do you think of Missis So-and-So's eldest?" This is where "Fancy that!" came in so handy. Perhaps Missis So-and-So's eldest had upped and died, and "Fancy that!" was suitably draped in black; or perhaps Missis So-and-So's eldest had gone off with the lodger, and "Fancy that!" was another way of saying "I knew it all along"; but "Fancy that!" it always was. As for "What's yours, ducks?" Ma B. was no snob. "What's yours, ducks?" had a universal quality about it; it applied equally to 225-pound dockers, vicars, tram drivers, kids, and dogs. Danny had a theory that Ma B. had eaten so much of her own suet puddings that her vocal chords had got gummed up and the only two utterances that could find their way out were "Fancy that!" and "What's yours, ducks?"

Ma B.'s pudding shop sold every kind of pudding; meat puds, suet puds with or without fruit, dumplings with or without fruit—every conceivable kind of thick pudding, Ma B. sold. As an incentive to buy her wares, the sauces were free: jam sauce, chocolate sauce, custard, and gravies of all sorts in great cauldrons. The only time that this suet pudding heaven-of-happiness was ever marred (and it happened two or three times an hour) was when some little urchin tried to swipe a free bit of pudding. Ma B. shifted her 280 pounds and brought the ladle down with a crash, but the little hand had long since gone. Ma B. wasn't a very good shot with her ladle. Not only did the waving of this lethal weapon shower everybody with custard or whatever sauce she had last used it for, but the blow often landed on and did some lasting damage to an innocent suet pudding on the counter. Those in the know stood well back or even sat at the SEATING PROVIDED FOR area, as the notice on the shop window read.

The evening of the arrested raisin pudding, we were seated at the tables. There were six of us. Anna and her two special buddies, Bom-Bom and Tick-Tock; Danny, a young French Canadian; Millie, the Venus de Mile End; and me. We'd got through our peas pud and steak and kidney pud and we were on to the raisin pudding course when the table next to us was occupied by two young men in uniform—French sailors. I don't know what led up to the remark, nor will I vouch for its complete accuracy, but suddenly: *"Mon Dieu,"* said the sailor, *"le pudding, il est formidable!"*

Anna's spoon stopped in midair. The mouth, open to receive the raisin pudding, opened further with astonishment; eyes that had been glazed with gustatory pleasure were suddenly pried wide open with question marks.

Danny answered the unasked question. " 'S French," he said, with his mouth full.

"What's he say?" asked Anna in a whisper.

"He said the pudding was 'orrible," laughed Bom-Bom.

But this was no time for jokes, and Anna did not join

in the general laughter. She lowered her spoon to the plate, and as if some colossal offense had been made against her, she said, "But I don't know what he's talking about."

Now my French is limited to *papillions* being *belle, vaches* eating grass, and the *pleur* being wet. In spite of this, I managed to tell Anna that French was spoken in France, that France was another country, and was generally that way, waving my hand in an eastward direction. I managed to convince her that this was no visitation of angels speaking the language of heaven, and that in fact Danny could speak French as well as he could speak English. She digested this bit of information more readily and easily than she digested Ma B.'s raisin pudding.

"Can I ask him?" she whispered.

"Ask him what?" I queried.

"To write what he said?"

"Sure."

With paper and pencil at the ready Anna went off to ask the sailor to "write it down big—about the pudding." Happily, one of the sailors spoke English, so she didn't need my help. Two cups of tea later she came back to our table and even managed an *"au revoir"* in response to their leaving.

The excitement of this meeting lasted for a day or two. The fact that there were more people in France speaking French than there were people in England speaking English was a bit of a shock.

A few days later I took her to the public library and showed her textbooks of various languages, but by this time Anna had distilled her astonishment and had tucked it in an appropriate corner of her mind. As she explained to me later, it was not really surprising when you got to think about it; after all, cats speak cat language and dogs speak dog language and trees speak tree language. So it wasn't really surprising that the French people spoke the French language.

I had been a little taken aback at Anna's reaction to hearing the French language spoken. She certainly knew of other languages; she could speak rhyming slang and back slang, and used a lot of Yiddish words in her own speaking. She was able to talk to Tick-Tock in sign language. This was necessary since Tick-Tock had been born deaf and dumb. Braille had intrigued her, and my own interest in ham radio had revealed to her the mysteries of the Morse code. What I did not know at the time of this French encounter was that she was already immersed in the problem of languages. Her reaction to the French language had been more on the lines of "What, another one?"

It seems that two questions had germinated in her mind concerning language. The first was Can I make a language of my own? The second was Just what is a language? The first question was well on the way to being solved. One evening I was shown the "working out" of this adventure. One of the many shoe boxes was taken from the cupboard and placed on the kitchen table; it contained notebooks and many sheets of paper.

The first sheet of paper to be taken from the box showed a simple column of numbers on the left-hand side of the page, and on the right-hand side, the word or words corresponding. The fact that it was possible to write "5 apples" with a numeral and "five apples" as a word was, I was told, very important. If all numerals could be written as words, then it followed that all words could be written as numerals. A simple substitution of the first twenty-six numbers in place of the twenty-six letters obviously did the trick, but writing *God* as "7.15.4" really didn't help very much.

Objects could be used as substitutes for letters or the names of the objects could be used. A reading primer had shown that "A is for Apple," and of course the implication was that Apple is for A. If Apple is for A, and Pear is for P, and Lemon is for L, and lastly, Elephant is for E, then the word *Apple* could be represented with the line of objects—Apple, Pear, Pear, Lemon, Elephant.

Sheet after sheet of paper showed that Anna had experimented with words, numbers, objects, and codes until she had finally come to the conclusion that the problem about inventing a language wasn't that it was very difficult; far from it. The difficulty was, how do you choose among so many possibilities? What she did come up with, however, was an adaptation of the Morse code. As this consisted only of dots and dashes, it was pretty plain to see that any two distinct things could be used. As Mister God had been thoughtful enough to provide a left foot and a right foot—well, these could be used to talk with. A hop on the left foot was to be taken as a dot, a hop on the right foot as a dash. Both feet on the ground was the end of a letter. We got quite good at this kind of communication and could converse over quite large distances. For close work the scheme was adapted to treading on a line of a paving stone for a dot and treading in the middle of the stone for a dash. By holding hands and pressing either with the little finger or the thumb, we developed a very intimate and private means of conversing. In all, Anna produced nine different variations of this system.

I got caught up with her enthusiastic approach to this

form of communication and produced two buzzer belts. The buzzer belt was simply a belt with two buzzers riveted on to it. When the belt was worn, one buzzer snuggled under the left ribs and the other under the right ribs. The serious drawbacks to this method were, firstly, that the buzzers tickled and made her laugh; secondly, that the whole business of being wired up with bell-pushes, batteries, and connecting wire was a bit tedious; and thirdly, that the first time we used it in the street we managed to trip up a couple of innocent people who, to say the least of it, were not amused—but definitely not— so we scrapped that method.

The question, Just what is a language? was a little more tricky to work out. In the course of her workings out, Anna had come to the conclusion that in the realm of numbers there was one number which was far more important than any other number. This was the number 1 —important because any other number could be made up by adding sufficient numbers of ones. True, there was a tricky way out. You could, of course, use signs like 5 or 37 or 574 instead of saying, "One plus one plus one plus one," etc. This method merely saved you time; it didn't alter the argument that 1 was the most important number. Like numbers, words also had a most important word and this word, naturally enough, was *God*. Anna saw the "most important number 1" as the apex of a triangle—only her triangle was standing on that apex! Number 1 had to bear the *weight* of all the other numbers.

Words were different. Words seemed to stand on piles of other words. These other words served the purpose of explaining the use and the meaning of the word on the top. The word *God* stood on the top of the pile that contained all the other words, and somehow or other you were expected to climb to the top of this pile to under-stand the meaning of the word *God*. This was a daunting idea. The Bible, the Church, the Sunday school were all busy building this colossal mountain of words and it was doubtful if anyone could climb to the top of such a pile.

Fortunately, good old Mister God had, in his wisdom, already solved the problem for us. The solution of the problem did not lie with *words* but with *numbers*. The number 1 bore the weight of all the other numbers, so it must be wrong to expect words to bear the weight of the meaning of the word *God*. No! It must be that *God* is the word that bears the weight of all the other words. So the pyramid idea of words with *God* on the top is *wrong side up;* so turn it *upside down.* That's better. Now the whole pyramid of words is standing on its apex like the numbers. The apex of the word *pyramid* is *God,* and that must be right because now the word *God* carries the weight and meaning of all the other words.

Anna showed me her workings out. One sheet con-tained an upside-down triangle standing on the point labeled 1—this was the numbers triangle. One sheet showed a triangle standing on the point labeled GOD, and the last sheet in the shoe box showed a triangle standing on the point marked ANNA!

"Ha," I said, "you've got a triangle all to yourself, I see!"

"No. Everybody has got one."

"Oh. What's it mean then?"

"It's for when I die and Mister God asks me all them questions."

"What about it?"

"Well, I've got to answer them all by myself. Nobody can do it for me."

"I see, but what does the triangle mean?"

"That I have got to be—"

"Responsible?" I suggested.

"Yes, responsible."

"Yes, I see. You mean you've got to bear all the weight like those other triangles do?"

"Yes, of the things I've done and the things I've thought."

Each word was underlined with a nod of satisfaction. She left me in the silence of her full stop.

It look a little time for all this to sink in, but it was true. We've all got to bear the weight of our own actions. We've all got to be responsible—either now or later. We've got to answer Mister God's questions all by ourselves.

FOUR

There was no doubt about it, Anna's arrival had caused a fair degree of upheaval in the house, given me lots of problems to deal with, and caused a lot of heartache. From the very beginning I had seen her as someone who was a little unusual. Perhaps it had just been the unusual way we had met. The first few weeks had shown me that she was certainly no baby angel, no changeling, in fact not even a sprite. No, she was at least a hundred percent child, complete with the giggles, dirty face, and breathless wonder. She went flat out after each day, as busy as a bee, as inquisitive as a kitten, and as playful as a puppy.

I suppose to some extent all children have a touch of magic about them—like some mysterious living lens, they seem to have the capacity to focus the light into the darkest and gloomiest of places—and this one had it in a very high degree. Perhaps it's the very newness of the young, or perhaps it's just because the shine hasn't worn off, but they can and do (if you give them half a chance) make a dent in the toughest armor of life. If you're very lucky they can dissolve away all those protective barricades so carefully erected over years of living. Lucky, did I say? Well, if you can take in your stride being twenty years of age and naked, then you are lucky. If you can't, then it's hell. I've seen other people knocked right back on their heels at some of Anna's comments. It wasn't that her remarks were all that clever and penetrating, it was just that she made herself so vulnerable. This made people hesitate as to the next step. This was a trick that she had learned: make people hesitate by whatever means you have at your disposal, fair or foul. And Anna was not above using tricks if they achieved her aim. Make people hesitate, and your remarks have a better chance of being looked at, being seen again. I suppose on the whole I didn't do too badly, considering. I didn't give in without a struggle. Letting your soul, or whatever fancy name you like to give it, out of its cage and into the daylight is perhaps the hardest thing anyone can do.

The hoarding down the Broadway displayed in large red lettering: DO YOU WANT TO BE SAVED? I wondered just how many people would say yes to that. Had it read "Do you want to be safe?" millions of people would have said "Yes, yes, yes, we want to be safe," and another barricade would have gone up. The soul is imprisoned, protected, nothing can get in to hurt it, but then it can't get out either. Being *saved* is nothing to do with being *safe*. Being *saved* is seeing yourself clearly —no "bits a colored glass," no protection, no hiding— simply seeing yourself. Anna never said anything about being saved, never to my knowledge attempted to save anybody. I don't suppose she would have understood this way of putting things, for this was my interpretation. But Anna knew full well that it was no use playing things safe; you simply had to "come outside" if you wanted to make progress. "Coming outside" was dangerous, very dangerous, but it had to be done; there was no other way.

It wasn't very long after Anna had come to live with us that I tried to tie a label on her. I suppose it was for my own satisfaction and comfort, but thank God she wouldn't stay labeled. After the first few weeks of delicious enchantment with Anna I found myself faced with two problems, one of which was fairly immediate and easy to understand; the other grew more slowly and was very difficult to understand. Neither of these problems was easily solved, in fact it was over two years before I felt that I had the answers. The solution to both problems came at the same instant.

My first problem was, exactly what was my relationship with Anna? I suppose I was old enough to be her father, and for some time I wore that role without any great success. Perhaps the part of a big brother was a better bet, but that didn't fit either. I saw myself variously as father, brother, uncle, friend. Whatever I called myself seemed to leave an emptiness which needed to be filled. Nothing happened for a long time.

The other problem was, what exactly was Anna? A child certainly, a very intelligent and a very gifted child, but what was she? Everybody who came into contact with Anna recognized in her some strangeness, something that marked her as different from other children. "She's fey," said Millie. "She's got the 'eye,'" said Mum. "She's a bloody genius," said Danny. The Reverend Castle said, "She's a very precocious little girl." This certain strangeness in Anna gave some people an uneasy feeling, but her innocence and sweetness acted like a balm, soothing away suspicions and fears. Had Anna been a mathematical genius all would have been well; she could have been written off as a freak. Had she been a musical prodigy we could all have cooed with delight, but she was neither of these things. Anna's strangeness lay in the fact that her statements were so often right, and as time went by they became more and more often right. One of our neighbors was quite convinced that Anna could see into the future, but then Mrs. W. was like that. Mrs. W. lived in a world of tarot cards, tea leaves, and premonitions. The fact however remained that Anna was so often right in her predictions that she appeared to be some sort of diminutive prophet, or East End oracle.

Certainly Anna had a gift, but it turned out to be

nothing spooky, nothing out of this world. In a very deep sense it was at once as mysterious as it was simple. She had an immediate grasp of pattern, of structure, of the way that bits and pieces were organized into a whole. Unexplainable as this gift might be, it was always well and truly earthed in the nature of things. As simple and as mysterious as a spider's web, as ordinary as a spiral seashell. Anna could see pattern where others just saw muddles, and this was Anna's gift.

The day that the horse and cart got its back wheel stuck in the tram lines produced half a dozen willing helpers.

"All together, lads. When I say 'heave,' all heave together. Ready? Heave!"

We all heaved like mad. Nothing happened.

"Once again, lads. Heave!"

We all heaved once again; same result—nothing.

After a few minutes of heaving and cussing, Anna tugged at my coat. "Fynn, if you put something across the line under the wheel and something so it won't go

back again, and then push, it's easier, and the horse can help."

With the help of a flat iron bar and a few bits of timber we pushed and the horse pulled. The wheel came out as sweetly and as easily as a cork out of a bottle. Someone thumped me on the back. "Good lad, that was a good idea of yourn." How could I say that it wasn't my idea? How could I say it was hers? I just accepted the praise.

Yes, it was true, Anna certainly had a lot of luck. Such moments as these gave me great pleasure and pride in her achievements; but there were also moments of great anguish when she seemed to overstep the mark, moments when her remarks, her statements, her claims, seemed to me to be so rash, so wildly out, that I felt compelled to say something. She took it all without comment. I felt like a heel and I didn't get it right for a long time.

Now Anna accepted the concept of the atom as easily as a canary bird accepts birdseed; accepted the size of the universe and its billions of stars without batting an eyelid. Eddington's estimate of the number of electrons in the universe was admittedly a fairly large number, but nevertheless very manageable. It wasn't very hard to write down a number bigger than that, and Anna knew full well that numbers have the capacity for going on and on and on. Anna soon ran out of words to express very large numbers and this was becoming more and more important. The word *million* was adequate for most things, *billion* came in handy on occasions, but if you wanted to use a word for a very, very large number, well, you just had to invent one. Anna invented one: a *squillion*. A *squillion* was a very elastic sort of a word; you could stretch it as far as you liked. Anna was beginning to have need for such a word.

One evening we were sitting on the railway wall, just

watching the trains go by and waving to anyone who would wave back. Anna was drinking her "fissy" lemonade when she started to giggle. It's difficult to describe the next few minutes. If you want some kind of a picture, I suggest you try to drink fissy lemonade, giggle, and develop the hiccups. I waited until the giggles had died down, until the hiccups had stopped, waited until the toss of the head had settled her hair back into place.

"Well," I said, "what's so funny, Tich?"

"Well—I just thought I could answer a squillion questions."

"Me too," I replied, without any surprise.

"Can you do it too?" She leaned forward with excitement.

"Sure! Nothing to it. Mind you, I might get about half a squillion wrong." I'd taken careful aim with this remark, but it fell wide of the mark.

"Oh," the disappointment was obvious. "I get all my answers right."

This, I thought, is the time for a bit of the old guiding hand stuff; a bit of correction wouldn't come amiss.

"You can't. Nobody can answer a squillion questions right."

"I can. I can answer a squillion squillion questions right."

"That's just not possible. Nobody can do that."

"I can—I really can."

I took a deep breath and turned her to face me, quite ready to scold her. I was met by a pair of eyes, calm and certain. It was obvious that she thought she was correct.

"I can teach you," she continued.

Before I had a chance to utter another word she was off.

"What's one add one add one?"

"Three, of course."

"What's one add two?"

"Three."

"What's eight take away five?"

"Still three." I wondered just where this was getting me.

"What's eight take away six add one?"

"Three."

"What's a hundred and three take away a hundred?"

"Hold it, Tich! Of course that answer's three, but you're cheating a bit, aren't you?"

"No, I'm not."

"It looks like it to me. You're just making these questions up as you go along."

"Yes, I know."

"Why, you could go on asking that kind of question until the cows come home."

Her grin exploded into a roar of laughter and I wondered what I had said that was so funny. It was the tilt of the head and the grin that made me realize what I had said. If asking questions till the cows came home wasn't the same as a squillion questions, what was it? Just in case the lesson hadn't been rammed home far enough, she turned the thumbscrew one last turn with, "What's a half and a half and a half and a——" I put my hand over her mouth; I'd got the message. I didn't give the answer; I wasn't supposed to. With the ease and matter-of-factness that a mother shows when patting up baby's burps, she finished off with, "And how many question sums is *three* the answer to?"

Duly chastised, I answered, a little uncertain as to what garden path I had been led up, "Squillions."

By this time I had looked away and was busy waving to the passing trains as if nothing had happened. After a moment or two she put her head on my shoulder and said, "Ain't it funny, Fynn; every number is the answer to squillions of questions?"

I suppose it was at that point that my education began in earnest. For quite some time I just didn't know which way was up or down or if I was coming or going. I had been taught the good old-fashioned method of question first, answer second. Now I was being taught by a half-pint, redheaded demon that almost every sentence, grunt, number, or utterance was the answer to an unuttered question. I suppose it is possible to fault this method of approach, but now I'm stuck with it, and it's very usable. Very gently, but with great excitement, I was instructed in the method of walking backward. Keeping my eye firmly on the answer, I was encouraged to walk backward until at last I bumped into the question. Patiently, it was pointed out to me that the answer *three* was very important and useful because it led back to squillions of questions. The more questions an answer led back to, the more useful that answer was. The interesting thing about this method, I was told, was that some answers led back to a very few questions, and some answers led back to only one question. The fewer questions an answer led back to, the more deeply important were those questions. When an answer led back to only one question, then you'd hit the jackpot.

As I was slowly initiated into this upside-down world, I found myself positively enjoying the kind of answers that led back to squillions of questions. That the number *nine* stood as the answer to squillions of unasked questions I found myself getting more and more excited about. I too could answer squillions of questions right. In this aspect of the upside-down world I found myself somewhere near the top of the class, constructing questions of such complexity that I would have hesitated to try to solve them had I not known the answer from the beginning. At the other end of the scale, the end where an answer led back to only one question, I was at the bottom of the class. Uncertain, hesitant, and most unwilling to state the question.

Taking a stroll one evening with me and playing an unending solo game of hopscotch on the paving stones, Anna suddenly flung over her shoulder without stopping her game: "Fynn, say 'In my middle'."

As a very obedient pupil, I chanted, "In my middle."

From ten yards ahead of me she yelled, "Wot?"

I stopped dead in my tracks, filled my lungs with the necessary, and yelled, "In my middle."

Little old ladies with their shopping baskets hurriedly crossed over the road with sidelong glances at me. Young girls giggled and children made those sorts of signs that indicated that I had a screw loose somewhere. Whatever activities or thoughts these good people had been engaged in were rudely interrupted by a six-foot-plus, 225-pound young man suddenly standing still and yelling, fit to wake the dead, *In my middle*. Sympathetic looks and such remarks as "He must be bonkers," "You never can tell by looks, can you?" were aimed in my direction. How could they possibly have known that I was conversing with that leaping, prancing demon, that redheaded kid, now some thirty or forty yards away? Obviously the man was having some kind of a seizure. At all these reactions to my yell my mouth fell open and I gaped like a stranded goldfish, my eyes stood out on stalks. I must indeed have looked bonkers. With a flood of embarrassment I rapidly pulled up my anchors, slammed my legs into top gear, and fled down a side street, around the block, and braked hard in front of Anna, who was still spring-heeling it on the spot.

"Oi!" I panted. "You with me?"

My mentor—or was she my tormentor?—still continued with her demented yoyo act. I put both hands on her head and pressed her to a stop with, "Hold it; your engine's still running. Cease. You'll curdle your brains."

She ceased and said, "What's the *big* question, Fynn?"

"How the heck do I know?" I answered, looking back down the street, half expecting to see white-coated men bearing down on me with straitjackets.

"You're frightened." She took my hand and we went on our way. It wasn't an accusation, just a matter-of-fact observation. We came to the canal bridge and Anna said, "Let's go down to the canal." I picked her up and leaned over the bridge, holding her at arm's length, and dropped her the five feet or so on to the tow path. This was our usual method of getting down to the canal; we never ever used the stairs about twenty feet away. We mooched along down the tow path, said "How do" to a couple of horses, plopped a few stones into the canal, and sunk a baked-bean tin. We searched for a handful of skimming stones and skimmed for about half an hour, managed to bounce a few stones on to the opposite tow path with one bounce, and pressed on down the path. We came to a moored barge and clambered on board and sat up at the front end with our legs dangling over the side. I rescued a cigarette from my coat pocket and straightened out the kinks, searched for, and found, a match. Anna lifted up her foot and I scraped the match alight on the sole of her shoe. I lit the cigarette and took a long drag.

69

We lay there side by side on the barge, soaking up as

many ultraviolet rays as managed to stagger through the steam and smoke of the surrounding factories. I was dreaming of my nice white yacht sailing through the Mediterranean, the steward bringing me cool pints of bitter and lighting my specially made monogrammed cigarettes. The sun was shining in a clear blue sky and the fragrance of exotic flowers wafted across the waters. Beside me lay this enchanting child, happy and contented, radiating sweetness, as innocent as a summer's morning. Little did I know that this miniature angel was busy stoking up her question-and-answer boiler, waiting for a good head of steam. Little did I know that she was busy sharpening up her scalpels, saws, and cold chisels, weighting the haft of her sledgehammers. Halfway through my second glass of bitter my beautiful white yacht struck a mine and sank instantly. My comfortable couch was now the metal deck of a barge, my pillow a coil of tarred rope, my monogrammed cigarette was a dead and drooping butt, and the sweet smell of flowers wafting across the Mediterranean was the soap factory working overtime. The golden sun in the clear blue sky was peering watery-eyed through the sulfurous clouds from the chimney stacks.

"You empty in yer middle?"

I closed my eyes tightly, hoping that another yacht would pick me up. Already it was beginning to take shape. I could see the news placards: DRAMATIC SEA RESCUE, YOUNG MAN RESCUED AFTER 21 DAYS AT SEA— EXCLUSIVE STORY. I was beginning to like this; I fitted the part well.

"Oi!"

My right ear exploded and all my dreams fled out of my left ear. A good hard prod with an elbow and my empty brainbox filled up with reality again.

"What? What's up?" I said, prying myself up on to my elbow.

"You empty in yer middle." I didn't know if that was a question or a statement.

"Course I'm not empty in my middle."

"Wot's the question then?"

I thought that I knew what she wanted me to say, but I wasn't going to say it; she could stew. I chewed it over for a few moments and framed the question, "Where is Anna?" On second thought I decided that this particular question was a bit too dangerous, so I said, "Where is Millie?"

She grinned at me and I felt that at any moment she would pat me on the head and pop a sweetie into my mouth for the good little pupil that I was.

"And wot's the question to the answer, 'In Mill's middle'?"

Ha! I'd already worked that one out. A 24-carat, fool-proof question-stopper, a real doozie, one that she hadn't bargained on, one that she couldn't wriggle out of. With great care and deliberation I replied, "The answer, 'In Mill's middle' leads back to the question, 'Where is sex?',", and added to myself, "And now, you little perisher, get out of that!"

She didn't have to get out of it—she never got into it. Without the flicker of an eyelid, without the catch of a breath, she pressed on. Her questions and proddings were like the waves breaking on the seashore: as one rolled up the sandy shore, so millions of others were being formed far out at sea. They were rolling in relentlessly and nothing could stop them. So it was with Anna's questions and proddings. In the depths of her being questions were being formulated, boiling up to spill out of her mouth, out of her eyes, out of every action; nothing could stop them—but nothing. It was as if every occasion inside her was destined to meet its companion occasion outside her.

She started to say, "What is the question to the answer, 'In the middle of sex'?"

I reached out my hand and silenced her question with a finger on her lips. "The question is," I said, " 'Where is Mister God?' "

She bit my finger—hard—and looked at me. Her eyes said, "That's for keeping me waiting." Her lips said "yes."

I lay back again on the deck of the barge and thought about what I had said. The more I thought about it, the more did I come to the conclusion that it really wasn't bad at all—in fact it was pretty good. I liked it. At least it prevented all the fuss and bother of pointing up there and saying that's where God is, or pointing out among the stars and saying that God is there! Yes, indeed, I liked it very much—only—.

The *only* didn't get resolved for quite a few days. Even then "teacher" had to lead me gently by the hand and explain in words that this idiot could understand. You see, I had gotten to the point where I could, without any undue hesitation, give the question to the answers, "In the worm's middle," "In my middle," "In your mid- dle." I'd even stopped getting het up about the question to the answer, "In the tramcar's middle." The question was, "Where is Mister God?" So far so good. Everything in the garden was lovely, except perhaps for one tiny, irrelevant and unimportant fact. I was ringed about with an unclimbable, impenetrable, couldn't-see-the-top-of range of mountains.

The names of these towering peaks were: the worms in the *ground*; I'm *here*; you're *there*; the tramcars mov-

72

ing *down* the street. I had gotten stuck with all these multitudinous and varied things which had middles in which Mister God was! The whole universe it seemed was strewn and littered about with sundry *theres* and various *heres*. Instead of some whole and big Mister God sitting around in a heaven of umpteen dimensions, I was now faced with a vast assortment of little Mister Gods inhabiting the middles of everything! Perhaps all these middles contained bits of Mister God which had to be put together like some gigantic jigsaw puzzle.

After it had all been explained to me, my first thought was for poor old Mohammed. He had to go to the mountains, but not Anna. She neither went to the mountains nor did she fetch the mountain to her—she merely said "Scat." And they scatted. Mind you, although I knew by then that the mountains were not really there, and that I could move about freely and unhampered, there are occasions—not many, I'm glad to say—when I get the distinct feeling that I've been brought up pretty sharpish-like by a clunk on the head. It certainly feels as if I have walked into a mountain, even though I can't see it. Perhaps one day I shall be able to walk about freely, without ducking occasionally.

As for my problem about the *heres* and the *theres,* the explanation went like this:

"Where are you?" she had said.

"Here, of course," I replied.

"Where's me then?"

"There!"

"Where do you know about me?"

"Inside myself someplace."

"Then you know my middle in your middle."

"Yes, I suppose so."

"Then you know Mister God in my middle in your

middle, and everything you know, every person you know, you know in your middle. Every person and everything that you know has got Mister God in his middle, and so you have got his Mister God in your middle too. It's easy."

When Mr. William of Occam said, "It is vain to do with more what can be done with less," he had invented his famous razor, but it was Anna who sharpened it!

Trying to keep up with Anna and her ideas could be a very exhausting business, particularly because I had finished with my schooling, or so I thought. Here was I, all nicely stacked up with ideas of what was what, and I was being made to unstack them again; and sometimes it wasn't all that easy. Like the time I was introduced to the idea of sex!

One of the great advantages of living in the East End was sex. In those days it was spelled with a small *s* and not with a big *S*. By "advantage" I mean that nobody spent half their life wondering if they were born in a beehive or a bird's nest. The whole of the birds-and-bees saga was out, but definitely. Nobody was in any doubt as to their origins. One might have been conceived under a gooseberry bush, but born, never. Most of the kids were familiar with the good old-fashioned, four-letter, Anglo-Saxon words before they could even count to four or knew what a letter was. Those were the days when the said Anglo-Saxon words were used as nouns and verbs and not as adjectives; when sex with a little *s* was as natural in its right place as the air we breathe. It hadn't gotten the self-importance of a capital *S,* nor for that matter its problems. Perhaps it was because we learned about it so early on in our lives that it rarely got snagged up. Perhaps it's only when you learn about it late in life that you begin to spell it with a capital

S. This has nothing to do with sex with a small *s* or a capital *S.* This has to do with Anna's discovery of *SEX,* the kind that you spell with all capitals.

It wasn't that there was anything wrong with the ordinary run-of-the-mill sex stuff, it was all perfectly understandable. After all, babies were babies, whatever else you called them. Kittens are babies, lambs are babies; and what about baby cabbages? One thing they all seemed to have in common was the fact that they were new, brand new; they were, as Anna said, "borned," or in other words, had been brought forth! If this were true, and it certainly appeared to be true, then what about ideas, what about stars, what about mountains, and suchlike? You couldn't argue with the statement that words brought forth new ideas. Could it be that words had something to do with sex? I don't know how long Anna had been mulling over this problem; it may have been for months. One thing was certain: she hadn't sorted anything out, otherwise I would have had the full blast of her discoveries.

It was a happy coincidence that I happened to be around when she made her breakthrough. It happened one Sunday afternoon after a not-very-successful Sunday school meeting. Danny and I were holding up the lamppost, chatting to Millie. The street was full of kids playing high-jimmy-knacko and skipping games, and four or five of the little ones were playing with a yellow balloon. The balloon game did not last very long as a balloon is not made to withstand the combined weight of five kids lying on it. It burst. Millie charged off to mop up the tears and to give general comfort to one and all. Danny was roped into being the cushion for the next team to be "downsy" in the high-jimmy-knacko game. Anna had stopped the never-ending chant of a ball-bouncing game and had picked up the burst balloon. She drifted over toward me and sat on the curb by the lamppost. In a kind of reverie she was pulling the remains of the balloon into various shapes.

Suddenly I heard it. It was the sound of Anna's tongue slapping against the back of her teeth; it was a sign that her thinking apparatus was working overtime. I looked down. Anna had gotten one end of the burst balloon trapped by her foot to the pavement. While she was stretching it with the one hand, she was poking it with her right index finger.

"That's funny," she murmured. Her unblinking eyes solidified this experiment like some twentieth-century Medusa.

"Fynn?"

"What's up?"

"Will you pull this for me?"

I got down beside her and was handed the burst balloon.

"Now pull it for me."

I stretched the balloon for her and she stuck her finger into it.

"That's funny."

"What's funny?" I asked.

"Wot's it look like?"

"Looks like you're sticking your finger into a burst balloon."

"Don't it look like a man's bit?"

"I suppose it does, kind of."

"Looks like a lady's on the other side," she said.

"Oh! Does it? Let's have a look." I looked, and it did

in a way.

"That's funny, that is."

"Well, what's so funny about it?"

"If I only do one thing," she poked her finger into the balloon again, "it makes a lady's and a man's. Don't you think that's funny, Fynn? Eh?"

"Yes. Two for the price of one. That's funny."

She went off to play with the other kids.

It must have been about three o'clock in the morning when she stood beside my bed.

"Fynn, you awake?"

"No."

"Good, I thought you were asleep. Can I come?"

"If you want to."

She slid into bed.

"Fynn, is church sex?"

I was awake, very much so!

"What do you mean, is church sex?"

"It puts seeds in your heart and makes new things come."

"Oh!"

"That's why it's Mister God and not Missis God."

"Oh, is it?"

"Well, it might be. It might be." She went on, "I think lessons is sex too."

"You'd better not tell Miss Haynes that."

"Why not? Lessons put things in your head and some new things come."

"That's not sex, that's learning. Sex is for making babies."

"Not always, it ain't."

"How d'you make that out?"

"Well, if it's on one side, it's a man; if it's on the other side, it's a lady."

"One side of what?" I asked.

"I don't know. Yet." She paused for a few moments. "Am I a lady?"

77

"Almost, I reckon."

"I can't have babies though, can I?"

"Well, not quite yet."

"But I can have new ideas, can't I?"

"You sure can!"

"So it's like having a baby—a bit—ain't it?"

"Could be."

The conversation stopped at this point and I lay awake for about thirty minutes or so and then must have fallen asleep. Suddenly I was being shaken and Anna was asking me, "Asleep, Fynn?"

"Not now, I'm not."

"If it's coming out, it's a lady, and if it's going in, it's a man."

"Is it?—What is?"

"Anything."

"Oh, that's nice."

"Yes! Ain't it exciting?"

"Breathtaking."

"So you can be a man and a lady at the same time."

I got the idea that she was trying to put over. All the universe has got a *sex*-like quality about it. It is seminal and productive at the same time. The seeds of words produce ideas. The seeds of ideas produce goodness knows what. The whole blessed thing is male and female at one and the same time. In fact, the whole thing is pure *sex*. We've taken one aspect of it and called it *sex,* or made it self-conscious and called it *Sex*. But that was our own fault, wasn't it?

FIVE   The first two years with Anna were for
me years of pleasure, years of pride, and
of amusement, in the things she had said
and done. People often said, "Guess what Anna said today," or "Guess what Anna did this morning," and I'd
chuckle at the audacity of the child. The gap of years that
separated Anna and me was a good place to laugh from.
That laughter was warm and loving. That laughter was,
after all, a little higher up the ladder of understanding,
and one can afford to be generous from these high places.
The ladder was crowded; we were all forging ahead for
one reason or another. We had all of us wrestled with our
various problems; we had solved them to some extent. Of
course we could chuckle, of course we could be generous.
We could, from our elevated position, give advice to those
struggling below.

These were the first two years, though they weren't
wasted years. Anna cast her pearls about and I picked up
a good many, but not all of them. I left too many of them
lying about, and the feet of thirty years have trodden
them into the ground. I'm told that every second of our
life is somehow registered in our brains. I find that a
comforting thought, but in what chamber, in what con-
volution, do these pearls lie? I've never found the key
to unlock these memories, but sometimes it happens. I
find another pearl—some happening or some word—and
the memory comes back.

I shudder to think that for two years I was content to
eat the stale bread of learning, when right under my nose
Anna was busy baking new and crusty ideas. I suppose
I thought that a loaf ought to look like a loaf. To me
loaf and *bread* were synonymous, and at that time I hadn't
the sense to see the difference. In some part of my mind
I can still detect a feeling of shame, a flicker of anger, and

a sense of wasted time, from that moment when I realized that the important word was *bread*—that bread could be baked into an infinity of shapes. I hadn't the sense to see that the shape of the loaf had nothing to do with the food value of the bread. The shape was nothing but a convenience. But my education had been too much concerned with the shapes. At odd moments I find myself angered when I ask the question, "How much of what I was taught was a matter of convenience?" But I ask nobody. There's nobody there to give me an answer. What a stupid waste of time even to ask such a question. The answer lies ahead of me, not behind me. Anna has left her map of discovery behind, some parts pretty thoroughly explored, some parts only hinted at, but most parts of the map have arrows of direction on them.

The evening I discovered the nature of my relationship to Anna was the same evening I began to grasp what she was, or at least to see the way she worked.

It was early winter and dark. We had the kitchen to ourselves, and the shutters were closed. The gas lamp hissed its light into the room, the kitchen range, newly banked up with coal, spluttered its erratic candles of flame through the fire bars. On the kitchen table were a half-finished radio set, boxes of bits and pieces, a methylated spirit lamp, a soldering iron, and a clutter of tools, valves, and what have you. Anna was kneeling on a chair, elbows on the table, her chin resting in her cupped hands. I was at the opposite side of the table, my attention divided, like all Gaul, into three parts: the radio set I was making, Anna, and the shadows on the wall. As the coal in the kitchen grate warmed up, the trapped gases escaped and ignited. The brilliant flame imprinted Anna's shadow on the wall, exhausted itself, and went out; another took its place and cast another shadow.

The explanation was simple enough, but the effect somehow defied the explanation. The shadow was there by the picture, then it was there by the doorway, then there on the curtains. The shadow pulsated in the flickering flame as if it had a life of its own; it vanished and appeared somewhere else. There was no movement between one position and another. It came and went. It looked—how can I say it?—it looked as if the shadow was playing. My eyes moved from one shadow to another, then to three at the same time, then nothing. A few seconds later two shadows. Something itched deep inside me, but too deep to look at. Anna looked up, saw, and grinned. The merry-go-round inside me twirled, but nothing happened. Whatever had nudged had disappeared, leaving behind a hole in some part of me.

The radio grew bit by bit in silence, except for the sizzle of the soldering iron as it was plunged into the flux. Tests were made and at last the valves were plugged in and the batteries connected. A last look, and we switched on—nothing! It was just one of those things which happen from time to time. The meter set to the right voltage range, one or two measurements—ah! That's probably the fault. Unsolder this, set the meter to current reading, insert the meter into the circuit, switch on. Of course it was one of those silly mistakes, soon rectified. Anna's hand was on mine, her brow furrowed in thought.

"What you done with that?" She pointed to the meter.

"I've just found out what is wrong."

"Please do it all again," she wasn't looking at me, her eyes were riveted on the meter, "from where you used that just now."

"D'you mean put the fault back after I've taken all this trouble to find it?"

She nodded. So I put the fault back.

"Now what?" I asked.

"Now do wot you did before, but talk," she commanded.

"But, sweetie," I cried, "if I talk about what I'm doing, you won't be able to understand a word."

"Don't want to understand no words. It's somfink different."

"First I set this meter to read voltage on this range, then I attach the meter across this resistance to measure the voltage at this point." My finger stabbed at the various bits as I spoke their names. "Now we move on down to here and do the same thing all over again, and the meter registers the right voltage."

Getting to the faulty part, I hooked up the meter and Anna noted that the meter reading was very different.

"That's where it is," I exclaimed. "Now if I unsolder this bit here and put the meter to read current, we'll just see what happens."

I unsoldered, saying, "Now we put the meter in the circuit and, Bob's your uncle, no current."

The hands came forward again and I nodded. She unhooked the leads carefully and slowly hooked them back again. No current. Replacing the faulty part, I switched on again, made a few adjustments, and listened to the music.

Sometime after two o'clock in the morning I was wakened by the *clack, clack* of the curtain rings. By the light of the streetlamp I could see Anna standing there. It was strange how the noise of those curtain runners always kicked me wide awake; strange, considering the fact that we almost slept on the railway lines, with express trains running in one ear and out of the other, but the slightest jiggle of those runners and I was wide awake. After two years Bossy and Patch had elected themselves as Anna's bodyguard, a kind of advance guard scouting out possible danger that might harm their little mistress. Boss, the old show-off, always way out in front, had already landed on my chest, while Patch, with lesser courage, excused himself by continually looking back to see if Anna was still coming.

"You awake, Fynn?"

"What's up, Tich?"

"Full up!"

"Oh."

A little sob brought the guards tramping up my chest in order to size up the situation.

The sniffs lasted a few moments longer while I thumbed through the events of the last day or so, trying to figure out the possible reason for the tears.

"Did you put it in the middle?" she asked at last.

"Did I put what in the middle?"

"That bit at the end, when you undid it."

"Oh yes, I remember. When I unsoldered the circuit."

"Yes. Did you put the box in the middle?"

"Yes," I said, getting the drift of the conversation, "I suppose it was like putting it in the middle. Why?"

"Well, it's funny."

"Hilarious," I admitted. "But how is it funny?"

"Like church and Mister God."

"Oh sure, that is funny, that is."

"But it is. True. It is."

At two o'clock in the morning my brain cogs are apt to be a little slow in reacting. Obviously this was one of those times. Fueling up to meet this situation meant getting up, and it was too darn cold, so I lit a cigarette. The fumes hit my brain and I coughed awake my engine. I put my brain into bottom gear, church and Mister God being like repairing a radio was obviously going to be a tough hill to climb, and at that time in the morning I wasn't at all sure where my brakes were. Nothing was going to stop it, so resigning myself to the inevitable, I invited her to proceed with, "All right, so going to church is like mending a radio. I agree. I agree, only tell me about it slowly—nice and slowly."

"Well, first you put the box outside, then you put the box inside. That's like people in church: they keep outside and they ought to go inside."

"I wish you'd tell me exactly what's happened. Thin it out a bit so I can understand."

Her body relaxed as her mind sorted out suitable and simple phrases, easy enough for an adult to understand.

"When you first done it with the box. Why?"

"To measure the voltage."

"Outside?"

"Of course. You measure voltages outside the circuit."

"Then the last time you done it?"

"That was to measure current."

"Inside?"

"Yes, inside. You have to get inside the circuit to measure current."

"That's like people an' church, ain't it?"

She knew full well that I hadn't got it, so she continued.

"People," she paused to let this sink in, "when they go to church," another lengthy pause, "measure Mister God from the outside." She hacked at my shins with her toes in order to stress this point. "They don't get inside and measure Mister God."

She waited patiently, waited to see if these ideas had caught fire somewhere.

Out in the night the continental express hurtled its way

toward Liverpool Street Station and bed, its whistle shrieking out its desire for sleep. Flashing past our bedroom window, it dropped its whistle a couple of semitones, acknowledging my presence, hissing and laughing at my confusion. Sleepy Pullman cars chanted their lullaby—*diddle-didum, diddle-di-dee diddle-di-dee, suck it and see, suck it and see.* Everything was having a go at me this night. I did suck it and see. At least a couple of brain cells rubbed together and nudged the firefly of my imagination awake. Not enough to really see by, but something was there. I'd been reading Aquinas recently and he'd made no reference to "making a radio" so I asked him to move over a bit and make room for Anna. I asked a question here and there, and the answer gradually got pieced together.

As a supposed Christian you can stand outside and measure Mister God. The meter doesn't read voltages, it reads LOVING, KINDNESS, ALL-POWERFUL, OMNIPOTENT, etc. You have a nice lot of labels to stick about the place. So far so good. Now what's the next step? Oh yes, now I open up the Christian circuit and pop me, the meter, inside. Seems simple enough, nothing to it really—Hey, wait a blessed minute! Who was it that said, "Be like your heavenly Father"? Quiet that man, I've nearly solved the problem. If I'm inside the Christian circuit, then I'm a part of, *a real part* of Mister God, *a working part* of Mister God.

"You mean I can think I'm a Christian. I can measure God from the outside and say he's all-loving and all-powerful and all that, but really I'm a dead duck?"

"Them's just people's words."

86

"Sure, but I'm people."

"So you ought to know."

"What?"

"Them's just people's words."

I pressed on with, "So if I get into the circuit and measure Mister God that way, then I'm a real Christian?"

She waggled her head sideways.

"How come I'm not then?" I asked her.

"You might be like 'Arry boy."

"He's a Jew."

"Yes. Or like Ali."

"Here, hold on a bit, he's a Sikh."

"Yes, but it don't matter, if you measure Mister God from the inside."

"Slow down a bit. What the heck do I measure then, if I'm on the inside?"

"Nuffink."

"Nothing? How come?"

" 'Cos it don't matter. You're like a bit of Mister God. *You* said so."

"I never did say such a thing."

"You did, too. You said that the box is a part of it when you measure it from the inside."

It was true. I had said so.

So far as Anna was concerned, one thing was absolutely certain. Mister God had made everything, there was nothing that God hadn't made. When you began to see what it was all about, how things worked, how things were put together, then you were beginning to understand what Mister God was.

Over the last few months it had begun to dawn on me that Anna's real concern had very little to do with properties. Properties had the rather stupid habit of waiting upon circumstances. Water was liquid except, that is, if it was ice or steam. Then the properties were different. The properties of dough were different from the properties of bread. It depended on the circumstances of baking. Not for one moment would Anna have relegated properties to the dustbin. Properties were very useful, but since properties depended on circumstances, the roadway after the pursuit of properties was unending. No, the proper thing to pursue was functions. Being outside Mister God and measuring him gave you properties, seemingly an unending list. The particular choice of properties that you made produced that particular kind of religion that you subscribed to. On the other hand, being inside Mister God gave you the function, and then we were all the same: no different churches, no temples, no mosques, etc., etc. We were all the same.

What's the function, did you say? Oh, the function of Mister God is another one of those simple things. The function of Mister God is to make you like him. Then you can't measure, can you? As Anna said, "If you are, you don't know, do you? You don't think Mister God knows he's good, do you?" Anna's opinion of Mister God was that he was a perfect gentleman, and no gentleman could possibly swank about being good. If he did, he wouldn't be a gentleman, would he? And that would lead to a contradiction. It stands to reason, doesn't it? I know that daylight brings questions with it, that it's easy to accept these things at night, in bed with a miniature angel by your side, but stay with it. The function of Mister God is to make you like him. The various religions merely measure the properties, or some of them, for you. It doesn't really matter what color you are, what creed you subscribe to; Mister God shows no preference in his function.

We didn't sleep any more that night, we just chatted about this and that.

"Miss Haynes."

"What's wrong with Miss Haynes?"

"Do-lally-tap. She's barmy."

"Can't be, she's a school-ma'am. You can't be a school-ma'am if you're do-lally."

"She is."

"What makes you think?"

"She said I can't know everything."

"Guess she's right."

"Why?"

"Suppose your noddle's not big enough."

"That's the outside."

"Pardon me. I forgot."

"I can know everything inside."

"Ah!"

"How many things are there?"

"Squillions."

"More than numbers?"

"No, more numbers than things."

"I know all the numbers. Not the names, that's outside; just the numbers, that's the inside."

"Yes, I guess so."

"How many squiggle waves on that 'cilloscope?"

"Squillions."

"You know how to make squillions?"

"Yes."

"That's inside."

"Suppose so."

"You seen them all?"

"No."

"No, that's the outside."

Bless the child, I couldn't tell her that she had just framed the question that had for so long bothered me: "Why can't I know everything?" Because it's obvious that no man can know everything, so why try? All the same. . . . We went on chatting. As the time trickled on, things began to happen to me. Certainties and doubts stacked themselves on top of each other. Questions were formed and discarded. I felt I was right, but I was afraid to let go. I juggled words into sentences, but each sentence made me vulnerable, and that wasn't good. If my guess was right, Anna would have to take the responsibility. The church clock down the road clapped out six o'clock. The question was there and I had to know the answer.

"How many things don't you tell me about?"

"I tell you everything."

"That the truth?"

"No," she said quietly and with some hesitation.

"Why's that?"

"Some of the things I think about is very—very—"

"Strange?"

"Um. You're not angry, are you?"

"No, I'm not angry a bit."

"I thought you would be."

"No. How strange these things?"

She stiffened up beside me, dug her fingers into my arm and defied me to contradict her.

"Like two and five equals four."

The world came undone at the seams. I'm right. *I'm right.* I knew exactly what she was talking about. With as much calm as I could muster, I gave away my secret.

"Or ten?" I asked.

For a moment or two she didn't move. Finally she turned her face to me and very quietly said, "You too?"

"Yeah," I replied, "me too. How did you find yours?"

"Down the canal, the numbers on the barges, in the canal. How'd you find yourn?"

"In a mirror."

90

"In a looking glass?" Her startled surprise lasted for about one second.

"A looking glass, like water, yes."

I could almost hear the chains falling off me.

"Did you ever tell anyone?" Anna asked.

"A couple of times."

"Wot they say?"

"Not to be silly. Not to waste time. Did you ever tell anybody?"

"Once. Miss Haynes."

"What she say?"

"I was stupid, so I didn't say it anymore."

We giggled together, both free, both now unfettered. We shared the same kind of world. We were warmed by the same kind of fire. We both stood on the same spot, on the same road, going the same way. Our relationship was now clear to me. We were fellow searchers, companions, like spirits. To hell with the profits, to hell with the gains! Let's go and have a look, let's go and find out. We both needed the same kind of food.

We'd both been told that *five* meant *five* and nothing else, but the figure 5 reflected in the water or a mirror was the figure 2. And this fact of reflection would produce some pretty curious arithmetics, and this is what fascinated us so much. Perhaps they were not of any practical use, but it didn't matter. *Five* meant what is usually meant by *five* only by usage and convention. There was nothing at all special about the figure 5. You could allow it to mean anything you liked as long as you stuck to the rules once you had made them, and you could go on inventing rules forever—well almost. So you see, we were wasting our time, but we didn't see it that way; we saw it as an adventure, something that had to be explored.

Anna and I had both seen that math was more than just working out problems. It was a doorway to magic, mysterious, brain-cracking worlds, worlds where you had to tread carefully, worlds where you made up your own

rules, worlds where you had to accept complete responsibility for your actions. But it was exciting and vast beyond understanding.

I wagged my finger at her.

"Five plus two is ten."

"Sometimes it's two," she replied.

"Or then maybe it's seven." Who the heck cares! There's squillions of other worlds to look at. We gasped to a stop.

"Tich," I said, "get up. I've got something to show you."

I grabbed the wing mirrors off the dressing table and we crept into the kitchen. I lit the gas. It was cold and dark but it didn't matter. Our inner fires were working overtime. I found a large sheet of white cardboard and drew a long, thick, black line on it. I hinged the two mirrors together and stood them upright like an open book. Between the open mirrors was the thick black line. I peered into the open mirrors and adjusted the angle.

"Look," I exclaimed, holding my breath.

She looked but didn't speak. I began to close the angle of the mirror very slowly and I heard her gasp. She looked some more and went on looking, and then all hell broke loose. Her boiler burst. I remembered well the feeling when I had first seen it. I got the mirrors flat on the table before it happened. She hit me like an express train. Her arms around my neck nearly strangled me. Her fingers dug holes in my back. She laughed and cried and bit me. We were a million years past the use of words. There wasn't one that fitted, anywhere near fitted that moment. We were both physically exhausted. Mentally and spiritually we hadn't touched down. We never did.

SIX Over a cup of tea we made plans. As soon as it was open we'd go to the market and buy a whole stack of mirrors from Woolworth's.

When we got to the marketplace the shops were still closed. The stall holders were assembling their displays under the flaring carbide lamps. The street was crisscrossed with shafts of good-humored abuse, instructions, and speculations as to the course of the day. Feet were stamped as if to kill the creeping insects of the cold. Oildrum braziers stood on their bricks bringing the tea water to the boil. The coffee stall breathed its perfume of hot dogs and coffee over the marketplace.

"A cuppa, two o' dripping and a cheesecake, guv," said the taxi bloke.

"I'll have a cuppa and a couple of sausages," said his mate.

"What's for you, cock?" It was my turn.

"Two cuppas and four hot dogs."

I slapped the money on the counter and got back the change, along with a handful of tea from the dripping counter. Anna stood grasping her mug in both hands, nose buried deep. Over the rim of the mug two smiling and blazing eyes sucked in everything. She couldn't hold her tea and the hot dogs at the same time, so I stuck them between the fingers of my left hand, ready when she wanted them. There was a space on the next stall to put my mug down while I jiggled out a cigarette onehanded. I tried to light a match by scraping it with my thumb. I never managed to learn that trick. The nearest I ever got was when the match head came off and stuck under my thumbnail. It lit then. It wasn't supposed to do that, and it hurt. Anna lifted up her foot and I lit up. The tempo was hotting up.

"Mind yer backs please! Mind yer backs!"

Like the bow wave from a passing ship, we all washed into the curb and washed back again as a horse and cart sliced its way through the mob, the horse steaming in the morning frost.

"Ernie!" yelled the lady in the leather apron. "Where the 'ell's them ruddy cabbages?" To anyone who cared to listen she added, "He'll be the death of me; he'll put me in my grave."

"Fat chance!" said someone.

The sandwich-board man arrived, announcing to all and sundry that THE END IS NIGH, and asked for a cup of tea.

"Blimey, the 'erald angel's here!"

"Here you are, Joe. Have a cup of wet-and-warm with me."

It was the taxi bloke.

"Fanks, guv," said the herald angel.

"Wotcha, Joe. Wot's the good news for today?"

"The end is nigh," moaned old Joe.

"You give me the flippin 'orrors."

"What was it last week?"

"Prepare to meet thy doom!"

"How the hell do you get all them messages?"

"He gets a telegram from St. Peter."

From the end of the counter a voice like a clap of thunder menaced all the company with, "Which of you sodden baskits pinched me sausages?"

"They're under yer flippin' elbow."

" 'Arry, mind yer language, ther's a nipper here!"

'Arry pushed away from the counter with a fistful of sausages in one hand and a pint-size mug in the other. The mug looked like an eggcup in his hand.

" 'Ullo, nipper. Wot's your name?" said 'Arry.

"Anna. Wot's yourn?"

" 'Arry. You on yer own?"

"No. With him," she nodded at me.

"Wot you doing down the road this time of the morning?"

"We're waiting for Woolly's to open," explained Anna.

"Wot you buying at Woolwerf's?"

"Some looking glasses."

"That's nice."

"Buying ten of them."

"Wot you want ten for?"

"So's we can see different worlds," said Anna.

"Oh," said 'Arry, none the wiser. "You're a proper caution, ain't yer?"

Anna smiled.

"Would you like a bar a chocklit?" asked 'Arry.

Anna looked at me and I nodded.

"Please, mister."

" 'Arry," corrected 'Arry, wagging a couple of pounds of forefinger.

"Please, 'Arry."

" 'Arfer!" yelled 'Arry over his shoulder. "Chuck us a couple a bars a chocklit."

'Arfer chucked and 'Arry caught.

" 'Ere you are, Anna, some chocklit."

"Thank you," said Anna.

"Thank you, wot?" 'Arry's voice curled up into a question mark.

"Thank you, 'Arry." Unwrapping one of the bars, she offered it, saying, "Have a bit, 'Arry."

"Fanks, Anna, I fink I will."

A couple of tree trunks stuck out with large hams on the ends. The hams opened and they turned out to be enormous bunches of bananas. He broke off an 'Arry-sized bit of chocolate.

"You like 'orses, Anna?" queried 'Arry.

Anna admitted to liking horses.

"You come along and look at my Nobby," invited 'Arry.

We went around the corner into a little side street and there was Nobby, a positively giant-sized shire horse, festooned with horse brasses, his coat shining almost as

brightly as the brasses around his neck. Nobby was feeding from what looked to me like a two-hundredweight coal sack slung around his neck. At 'Arry's approach Nobby snorted into his bag, and we were all covered with showers of chaff and oats. 'Arry opened his mouth and out poured a tornado of laughter and love. Five minutes ago 'Arry had threatened to bash someone's brains in over his sausages, and I reckon he could have managed four or maybe six fully grown men. Now he'd melted into some kind of fairy story giant for a little girl and a horse. Anna was given a handful of sugar lumps for Nobby.

" 'E won't hurt yer, Anna. 'E wouldn't hurt a fly, 'e wouldn't."

"Nor would you, 'Arry," I thought, "you big lummox."

Nobby's lips curled back, exposing a row of what looked like tombstones, then curled themselves over the sugar lumps which disappeared. After a few more minutes of horse talk 'Arry said, " 'Ere, Anna, you sit on Nobby and talk to 'im and I'll unload this lot. Then I'll drive yer to Woolwerf's in proper style."

Anna took off and landed on Nobby's back, transported by one of 'Arry's bunches of bananas. The princess was mounted on her charger. 'Arry unloaded. Crates and sacks were shifted like so many bags of feathers. When 'Arry had finished he lifted Anna on to the driving box and sat beside her, I sat on the tailboard. Anna was given the reins. With a couple of "gee ups" we were off. I don't suppose that Nobby needed to be told where to go; he knew his route like the back of his hoof. We didn't go through the marketplace since the cart was of the same generous proportions as Nobby and 'Arry, like a battleship with wheels on. We stopped at a corner.

"Woolwerf's," bellowed 'Arry and leapt down like Pavlova herself. "There y'are, Anna, Woolwerf's," he declared.

"Thank you, 'Arry," replied Anna.

98 "Fank you, Anna," he grinned.

"See you sometime," he yelled as he and Nobby turned

the corner. We often saw 'Arry and his horse Nobby after that.

The lady behind the counter at Woolworth's needed a little convincing that we really wanted ten mirrors, but she handed them over to us and aimed in my direction, "You must fancy yourself."

We hurried home with our prize and cleared the kitchen table. I hinged two mirrors together with glue and pieces of cloth, like the covers of a book. Anna brought out the large piece of cardboard with the thick black line drawn on it and placed it on the table. Our mirror book was opened up and stood on the cardboard, the hinge furthest away from the marked line, the near edges of the mirrors just cutting the line. I peered into the angle of the mirrors and adjusted them. The marked line and the two reflected lines made an equilateral triangle. Anna peered. I closed the angle slightly, the lines adjusted themselves and a square appeared. Anna stared into the mirror book.

"A bit more," she commanded.

I closed the angle a little more and she counted, "One, two, three, four, five. It's got five sides."

After a moment or two, "What's it called?"

"A pentagon," I answered.

The book closed a little more and I announced the shapes to be a hexagon, a heptagon, an octagon. I ran out of names after a decagon so we merely counted the sides and called them a "seventeen-agon" or a "thirty-six-agon." Anna thought it was a very strange and wonderful book. The more you closed it, the more complex were the figures; very strange to say the least. What was even stranger was that the book was just a couple of mirrors. But if you had a separate page for every different "agon" you were able to see, why then you were going to need millions of pages, no, squillions of pages. This was truly a magic book. Who'd ever heard of a book with squillions of pictures in it and *no pages?*

As we closed the book more and more, we ran into a snag. The mirror book was only open about an inch and we couldn't get inside to see what was going on inside the book, so we started from the beginning again. When we got to the umpteen-agon again we couldn't get inside. What to do?

Anna said, "When we get to a squillion-agon it's going to be a circle."

But how do we get inside? This little puzzle was solved after some thought and a lot of false trails. We scraped off some of the silvering from the back of one of the mirrors and made a circle of clear glass about the size of a penny. A spy hole. We could now look inside. It was true, a squillion-agon was going to be a circle. Already it was difficult to decide that what we saw wasn't a circle.

Then another snag cropped up: as we closed up the book we ran out of light to see things by. Anna wanted to know what we would see if the mirror book was tightly closed. That was a tricky problem. How to get light into a tightly shut mirror book.

"Can't we put a light inside the mirror book?" asked Anna.

We dismissed matches and candles and finally hit upon the torch. The torch was quickly dismantled and reassembled; wires were soldered to the bulb and to the battery. We put the bulb into the book. It was a bit too big, we still couldn't shut the book completely. The solution to this little problem was almost immediate. The two mirrors parallel to each other about a half an inch apart would give us a very good approximation. We set it up and draped a cloth over it so that the light couldn't get in around the edges. Anna looked through the spy hole and gasped, "There's millions of lights," she whispered, and with even more surprise, "Fynn, it's a straight line!"

It had surprised me ten years ago, so I was ready for this. I reached across her and very gently squeezed the two mirrors together along one side, about a fraction of an inch.

She leaped back, looked at me and said, "Wot you do?"

I explained to her how to squeeze one pair of edges together.

"It makes the biggest circle in the world," she exclaimed.

As she sat there with her eye fixed on the biggest circle in the world, I squeezed the other two edges together. The biggest circle in the world straightened up and bent the other way.

The mirror book opened and closed a hundred times a day. A myriad different things were placed in the angle of the mirror. Patterns were formed of unbelievable complexity, enough to startle anyone.

One afternoon something new happened. Anna wrote large capital letters on pieces of card and placed them in the angle of the mirrors, and got inside.

"That's funny." Her head swiveled to look into the right-hand mirror, then swiveled to look into the left-hand mirror, back again to the right. "That's very funny," she said to no one. "The next one is the wrong way round, but the next one's the right way round."

Some of the reflected letters were back-to-front while others were still the right way round. She discarded the back-to-front letters and was left with $A, H, I, M, O, T, U, V, W, X, Y$.

I slid into a chair beside her and casually riffled through the discarded letters until I found A. I put the card on the table beside her and bisected the angle of the *A* with a single mirror. Anna looked, and then took the mirror out of my hands and tried it herself. Then she tried the other letters. It absorbed her for about an hour and then she brought it out.

"Fynn, if the half in the looking glass is the same as the half on the table then the letter don't change. *O* is the funny one because you can halve it in lots of ways." Anna was coming to grips with the axes of symmetry.

This was a new game to play; these were new wonders to be seen. Some things turned inside out or at least left to right, some things didn't. We made a pocket-size mirror book with handbag mirrors donated by Millie and Kate, backed it with wood against possible accidents, and took it into the street. This little book went everywhere with us. We'd flop down in the road on seeing some unexpected structure in a paving stone and out would come the mirror book. Beetles were gently introduced into the mirrors, leaves, seeds, tram tickets. Why, you could spend the whole of your life doing this sort of thing. Colored bulbs were sandwiched in the mirror book and switched on, and we peered through the spy hole. Why, for a couple of bob we could outdo Piccadilly Circus, Blackpool, and Southend all combined. It was all very miraculous; not only miraculous but useful, because we could see both sides of an object at one and the same time—well, more or less. Anna wondered if we could see all around an object, so we made a cube of mirrors. One side was hinged with a spy hole and objects were hung in the center of the cube by a cotton thread. We had to put lights inside, as it was too dark to see and—"Well, I'll be darned!"—we could see all the way around.

I never counted how many mirrors we bought and used;

it must have been well over a hundred. All the Platonic figures were made out of mirrors, plus a few shapes that Plato never dreamed of. Ours were just that bit different; we got inside ours and saw things that language would be hard put to describe. We discovered a lot of crazy arithmetics that made sense as long as you were prepared to live with these mirror worlds. Admittedly, on this side of the mirror things got a bit tricky, but as long as you remembered you were doing mirror stuff, that was all that mattered.

We learned to draw, write, and do our sums on a pad of paper before us. The difficulty lay in the fact that we didn't look at the paper, we looked at the reflection of the paper in a vertical mirror. The tension was at times unbearable, the concentration was absolute, but we mastered it.

One evening it was suggested that the mirror book was something more: it was a miracle book. Mr. Weekley's dictionary told us that mirror came from the Latin *mirari*, "to wonder at," and that miracle came from the Latin *mirus*, "wonderful." We knew that Mister God had made man in his own image, so could it be? Was it possible?

"He might have made a big mirror, Fynn!"

"What would he want to do that for?"

"I don't know, but he might have."

"Could be."

"Perhaps we're on the other side."

"How come the other side?"

"Perhaps we're the wrong way round."

"That's a thought, Tich."

"That's why we get it all wrong."

"Yeah, that's why we get it all wrong."

"Like numbers."

"Like numbers?"

"Yes, the numbers in the mirror."

"How's that?"

"Them numbers in the mirror, them numbers is take-away numbers not 'add' numbers."

"Don't get you, Tich. What you driving at?"

Anna took a paper and pencil and wrote 0, 1, 2, 3, 4, 5.

"Them is add numbers," she pronounced. "If you put a looking glass on 0, then the numbers come out 5, 4, 3, 2, 1. They're take-away numbers."

I was following the argument so far. The reflected numbers were take-away numbers.

She continued, "People are take-away people."

"Hold it." I put out a hand. "I don't get this 'take-away' stuff."

She hopped off the chair and staggered back with an armful of books. Settling herself once again on the chair, she thumped the table once or twice. "That's 0," she informed me, "that's 0 and that is the looking glass."

"Right, I've got that bit, that's the mirror." I gave the table a thump. "So what's next?"

She placed a book on the table.

"That's add one," she explained, looking hard at me. I nodded. She placed a second book on top of the first.

"That's add two." I nodded some more.

"That's add three, that's add four." The pile grew higher and higher. When she was satisfied that I had grasped exactly what she was saying, an arm knocked over all the books and she swept them on to the floor.

"Now."

We were obviously coming to the difficult bit.

"Where," she asked, "is a take-away book?" The question was asked with hand on her hip and head tilted.

"Search me," I answered. "I haven't got it."

Again she thumped the table a couple of times. "Down there. It's down there."

"Oh sure," I replied, "it's down there." I had not much idea what *there* referred to, and said so.

"A take-away-one book is a hole as big as a book, and a take-away-two books is a hole as big as two books. It's not hard," she said.

It wasn't, not when you got the hang of things, so I plunged in with, "So a take-away-eight-books number is a hole, eight books big."

She continued on her tutorial way.

"If you've got a take-away-ten-books hole and if you've got fifteen add books, how many books you got?"

I began to tip the fifteen add books down the hole one by one and watched them disappear. I lost ten that way and ended up with five.

"Five," I announced, "but what's that got to do with take-away people?"

I shrank about four feet under her sympathetic gaze and just managed to stop myself falling down the take-away hole.

"If," she underlined, "people are looking-glass people, then they are take-away people."

It's all pretty obvious, so obvious that it would take an idiot not to see it! We all know that Mister God made man in his own image and images are found in mirrors. Mirrors turned you back to front or left to right. Images were take-away things. So putting it all together, Mister God *was* and Mister God *is* on one side of the mirror, Mister God was on the add side. We were on the other side of the mirror, so we were on the take-away side. We ought to have known that. When Mum puts the toddler down and backs off a few paces she does so in order to encourage the toddler to walk to her. So did Mister God. Mister God puts you down on the take-away side of the mirror and then asks you to find your way to the add side of the mirror. You see he wants you to be like him.

"Take-away people live in holes."

"Must do," I admitted. "What sort of holes?"

"Different holes."

"Ah well, that accounts for it. How they different?"

"Some big, some little," she continued, "all with different names."

"Different names—such as?"

She walked around the holes, reading off the names as she went, "Greedy, Wicked, Cruel, Liar," etc., etc. On our side of the looking glass the whole place was littered with holes of various depths with people living at the bottom. On Mister God's side were appropriate piles of whatever, ready to fill up the holes if only we'd got the sense to ask for them. The piles also had names like Generosity, Kindness, and Truth. The more you filled up your hole, the nearer to Mister God's side of the mirror you got. If you managed to fill up your hole and still have something left over, why then you were well and truly on the add side— Mister God's side. You'll understand of course that Mister God looks into his mirror and sees us all, but we can't see Mister God. I mean, after all, a mirror image can't *see* what's looking at it. As Anna said, "Your face reflection can't *see* you, can it?" Occasionally Mister God sees fit to do something about somebody's hole, he—well—he sort of fills it up for them. It was what we called a "mirror-cle"!

Mister God was never far from any conversation, and Mister God was certainly getting more and more amazing. The fact that he could listen to, let alone understand, all the different prayers in all the different languages was something to marvel at, but even this paled into insignificance when compared with the stack upon stack of miracles that Anna was finding. Perhaps the most miraculous of all the miracles was that he had given us the capacity to find out and to understand these miracles. Anna reckoned that Mister God was writing a story about his creation. He had got the plot all worked out and knew exactly just where it was going. True, we couldn't help Mister God with this part of his activities, but we could at least turn over the page for him. Anna was turning over the pages.

One day I was stopped by Sunday school Teacher. Sunday school Teacher asked me, no, told me, to instruct Anna to behave herself in the class. I asked what it was that Anna had done or had not done and was told: one, that Anna interrupted; two, that Anna contradicted; and three, that Anna used bad language. Anna could, I admit, use a pretty good cuss word at times, and I tried to explain to Sunday school Teacher that, although Anna sometimes used language badly, she never, in fact, used the language of badness. My arrow missed the target completely. I could well imagine that Anna had interrupted her and also that she had contradicted her, but she wouldn't tell me the circumstances of this episode. That evening I spoke to Anna on the subject. I told her that I had met Sunday school Teacher and told her what had been said.

"Not going to no Sunday school no more."

"Why not?"

" 'Cos she don't teach you nuffink about Mister God."

"Perhaps you don't listen properly."

"I do, and she don't say nuffink."

"You mean to say you don't learn anything?"

"Sometimes."

"Oh, that's good. What do you learn?"

"Sunday school Teacher is frightened."

"What makes you say that sort of thing; how do you know that she's frightened?"

"Well, she won't let Mister God get bigger."

"How is it that Sunday school Teacher won't let Mister God get bigger?"

"Mister God is big?"

"Yeah, Mister God is good and big."

"And we're little?"

"Right enough, we're little."

"And there is a big difference?"

"Yeah, and then some."

"If there wasn't no difference, it wouldn't be worth it, would it?"

This confused me a little. I suppose I must have looked a bit puzzled, so she came again, sideways this time.

"If'n Mister God and me was the same size, you couldn't tell, could you?"

"Yes," I said, "I see what you mean. If the difference is very big, then it stands to reason that Mister God is big."

"Sometimes," she cautioned.

It obviously wasn't as simple as that. In easy stages I was led to accept the fact that the bigger the difference between us and Mister God, the more Godlike Mister God became. At such a time when the difference was infinite, then would Mister God be absolute.

"What's all this got to do with Sunday school Teacher? She certainly knows about the difference."

"Oh yes," nodded Anna.

"So what's the problem?"

"When I find out things it makes the difference bigger, and Mister God gets bigger."

"So?"

"Sunday school Teacher makes the difference bigger but Mister God stays the same size. She's frightened."

"Hey, hold on a tick. How come she makes the difference bigger and Mister God stays the same size?"

I nearly lost the answer; it was one of those real "give-away" lines. Tossed off so quietly.

"She just makes the people littler."

Then she went on, "Why do we go to church, Fynn?"

"To understand Mister God more."

"Less."

"Less what?"

"To understand Mister God less."

"Wait a blessed minute. You're flipped!"

"No, I'm not."

"You most certainly are."

"No. You go to church to make Mister God really, really big. When you make Mister God really, really, *really* big, then you really, *really* don't understand Mister God—then you do."

She was just a little surprised and disappointed to learn that this was over my head, way over my head, but she explained.

When you're little you understand Mister God. He sits up there on his throne, a golden one of course; he has got whiskers and a crown and everyone is singing hymns like mad to him. God is useful and usable. You can ask him for things; he can strike your enemies deader than a doornail; and he is pretty good at putting hexes on the bully next door, like warts and things. Mister God is so understandable, so useful, and so usable, he is like some object—perhaps the most important object of all—but nevertheless an object and absolutely understandable. Later on you understand him to be a bit different, but you are still able to grasp what he is. Even though you understand him, he doesn't seem to understand you! He doesn't seem to understand that you simply must have a new bike, so your understanding of him changes a bit more. In whatever way or state you understand Mister God, so you diminish his size. He becomes an understandable entity among other understandable entities. So Mister God keeps on shedding bits all the way through your life until the time comes when you admit freely and honestly that you don't understand Mister God at all. At this point you have let Mister God be his proper size—and wham!—there he is, laughing at you.

SEVEN Anna got involved with everything and anything; her involvement was on such a deep level that very little ever frightened her. She was ready to meet everything on its own terms. At whatever level the thing existed, Anna would be there to meet it. Occasionally she'd run into a situation for which she had no adequate word. She'd invent one, either a brand-new one or she'd teach an old one to do a new trick—like the night she told me that "the light, it frays."

Of course I should have known that light frayed but I didn't, so I had to go out into the dark street, armed with a torch and a tape measure. With the aid of a nearby dustbin and the railway wall it was demonstrated to me that light really did fray. The torch glass measured four inches across. The torch was placed on the top of the dustbin and the beam directed on to the railway wall. We measured the patch of light; it was just over three feet across. The dustbin and the torch were moved back a few paces and we measured the patch of light again; it was over four feet six inches across. The light did indeed fray.

"Why, Fynn? Why does it do that?"

So we'd go indoors again and out would come the paper and pencil and I'd explain.

"Can't you make it so it don't fray?"

So we'd talk about reflectors and lenses. It got taken in, digested, stored in its proper place and poised against some unknown eventuality.

The mirror book had provided Anna with another technique for wringing out interesting facts, the whole business of turning the thing inside out, or left to right, or upside down. That some of her facts weren't facts but fantasy didn't matter a jot, since by this time Anna knew exactly and precisely what a fact was.

A fact was the hard outer cover of meaning, and meaning was the soft living stuff inside a fact. Fact and meaning were the driving cogs of living. If the gear of fact drove the gear of meaning, then they revolved in opposite directions, but put the gear of fantasy between the two and they both revolved in the same direction. Fantasy was and is important; it leads to heaven knows where, but follow it and see. Sometimes it pays off.

The mirror book turned things from left to right, so why not turn everything around the other way for a start? Newton had a law; so did Anna. Anna's law was: First turn it inside out, then turn it upside down, then back to front, and then side to side, and then have a jolly good look at it, and . . . "Fynn, do you know that *room* spelt backward is *moor?*" Well, a room is a particular space surrounded by walls, and a moor is a particular space not surrounded by walls, so it makes some kind of sense, doesn't it? And while we are on the subject of rooms: "Fynn, if you spell *roof* backward, it spells *foor*. Can I put an *l* in it and make it spell *floor?*" Well, I don't see why not. "Fynn, is a *rood* a window, because it's *door* spelt backward?" "Fynn, do you know that *lived* backward is *devil?*" "Do you know that *Anna* spelt backward is *Anna?*" All right, so it's all coincidence, it's not relevant. Perhaps not, but it's fun, and sometimes the most surprising things happen.

Words became for Anna living things. She took them apart and put them together again. She learned what made them tick. She made no great etymological discoveries but she learned words and how to use them. Anna also painted—not very beautiful pictures, I admit, but then she painted under a severe handicap. She'd paint a picture wearing colored glasses and then laugh at the result. And then, "Fynn, will you make my red glasses blue for me?" and she'd paint another picture. None of Anna's pictures ever hung on the wall; they were never meant to. They were explorations into looking. It was very rash to deny the possibility that a red rose might be able to see. It might, just might, be able to see through its red petals or its green leaves; and you had to find out what the world might look like, hadn't you?

Being a sum doer myself, I was very interested in Anna's approach to mathematics. It was love at first sight. Numbers were beautiful things; numbers were funny things; they were without a doubt "God stuff." As such, you treated them with reverence. God stuff behaved itself. True, God stuff was sometimes very difficult to grab hold of. Mister God had, it seemed, told the numbers just what they were and just how to behave. Numbers knew exactly where and how they belonged in the scheme of things. Sometimes it suited Mister God to hide his numbers in sums or in mirror books; and mirror books, as you know, could get pretty darned complicated at times.

The love affair with numbers soured a bit and, for a long time, I never knew why. It was Charles who put me on to the track of the explanation. Charles taught at the same school as Miss Haynes, and Miss Haynes taught sums. Anna's attendance at school was reluctant and not too frequent, as I was to discover later. At one of these sums lessons Miss Haynes had focused her attention on Anna.

"If," said Miss Haynes to Anna, "you had twelve flowers in a row and you had twelve rows, how many flowers would you have?" Poor Miss Haynes! If only she had asked Anna what twelve times twelve was she would have got her answer, but no, she had to start messing around with flowers and rows and things. Miss Haynes got an answer, not the one she expected, but an answer.

Anna had sniffed. This particular kind of sniff indicated the utmost disapproval.

"If," replied Anna, "you grewed flowers like that you shouldn't have no bloody flowers."

Miss Haynes was made of stern stuff and the impact of this answer left her unmoved. So she tried again.

"You have seven sweeties in one hand and nine sweeties in your other hand. How many sweeties have you got altogether?"

"None," said Anna. "I ain't got none in this hand and I ain't got none in this hand, so I ain't got none, and it's wrong to say I have if I ain't."

Brave, brave Miss Haynes tried again.

"I mean pretend, dear, pretend that you have."

Being so instructed, Anna pretended and came out with the triumphant answer, "Fourteen."

"Oh, no, dear," said brave Miss Haynes, "you've got sixteen. You see, seven and nine make sixteen."

"I know that," said Anna, "but you said pretend, so I pretended to eat one and I pretended to give one away, so I've got fourteen."

I've always thought that Anna's next remark was made to ease the look of pain and anguish on Miss Haynes's face.

"I didn't like it, it wasn't nice," she said, as a sort of self-inflicted punishment.

This sort of attitude to the Mister God stuff of numbers was almost unforgivable, and it rocked Anna more than somewhat. The final blow came in the street one summer evening. Dink was sitting on the doorstep doing his homework. Dink was about fourteen and going to the Central

School. Dink could score goals from impossible angles and could knock a sixer over the railway wall with one wallop, but Dink and math were strangers, pretty well.

"Silly bugger," said Dink.

"Wot's up, Dink?"

"This geezer's having a bath."

"Ain't Friday, is it?"

"Wot's Friday got to do with it?"

"Barf night."

"That's got nuffink to do wiv it."

"What's the geezer doing, Dink?"

"He's got both taps turned on and he ain't got the plug in."

"Strewth, some mothers do have 'em—and they live."

"We ain't got no taps on our bath. We keep it in the yard and fill it up with a bucket outa the copper."

"Wot you gotta do, Dink?"

"Find out how long the bath takes to fill."

"He'll never do it."

"Never?"

"He'll get his deaf a cold standing around in the nood."

"He's a twit."

"Let him barf 'imself. Have a game of footy, Dink. Dibs on being goalkeeper."

Anna had been listening to this exchange and it confirmed her worst fears. Sums were an invention of the Devil, they turned you away from the real God stuff of numbers and tied you up in a world of idiots.

It was just past knocking-off time and we had got the worst of the muck off our hands. Cliff and George and I were crossing the yard, heading for the gate, and there she was waiting. I broke into a run at seeing her—wondering. She ran to meet me.

"What's wrong, Tich? What's happened?" I asked.

"Oh Fynn," she threw her arms around me, "it's so lovely. I couldn't wait."

"What's lovely? What is it?"

Anna fished about in her pouch and thrust something into my hands: a sheet of graph paper, numbered in each square. It looked straightforward enough to me. The number in the top left-hand corner was 2. The numbers progressed across the paper: 1, 0, 1, 2, 3, 4, 5, 6, 7. The next line began 8, 9, 10, 11, etc. Six rows of numbers, ending up with 57 in the bottom right-hand corner of the page. It was a simple arrangement of consecutive numbers. Anna searched my face, waiting for it to light up. It didn't. It just registered puzzlement.

"I'll show you, I'll show you," she said excitedly.

We knelt there on the pavement, homeward-going workers making a detour around us with amused smiles on their faces. Anna traced around a large square made up of four smaller squares. The top two squares were numbered 22 and 23, the bottom two 32 and 33.

"Add those two," she commanded, pointing to the diagonal numbers, 22 and 33.

"Fifty-five," I obliged her.

"Now those two." She pointed at the other pair of diagonal numbers, 23 and 32.

"Fifty-five," I grinned.

"The same." She squirmed with delight. "Ain't it wonderful, Fynn?"

Next she traced a larger square made up of sixteen smaller squares. With two quick strokes of her pencil she divided sixteen into four squares each containing four of the smaller squares.

"And that lot and that lot." She pointed to the top left

group of four squares and the bottom right group of four squares.

"Now these," she said, indicating the top right group and the bottom left group. The answer was the same.

For the best part of thirty minutes we juggled with groups of squares. It was always the same. The group of numbers on one diagonal was the same as the group of numbers on the other diagonal!

It was obvious when you thought about it. One diagonal was the mirror image of the other diagonal, so it followed naturally that all the numbers on one diagonal were, in some mysterious way, the mirror image of all the numbers on the other diagonal!

Good old Mister God! He'd done it again!

Later that evening I was told that she had made scores of these arrangements, putting the o wherever her fancy led her. Also she had found some very complicated series, and it always worked. Mister God numbers, the real God stuff, was, as you might expect, a never-ending miracle. As for that other stuff, the bath-filling lark that Old Nick used numbers for—well—!

Anna's refusal to get involved in this "Devil stuff" in sum books was absolute. There was no power on earth, or for that matter in hell, that could make her. I tried to explain that all this devil stuff was simply a means of demonstrating the laws of what you could and couldn't do with numbers. I needn't have bothered. Anyhow, Mister God stuff told you what you could and couldn't do, too. Do you mean to tell me that you'd go to all the trouble to get two men to dig a hole in two hours and then—what do you do? You don't ask the proper question, "What are you digging the hole for?" No, you bring along another five men to dig the same size hole, just to find out how long it takes. The man in the bath? You can't tell me that you actually know anybody who would turn both the taps on and then deliberately leave the plug out. As for the rows of flowers, well. . . .

Anna never had any difficulty in separating the idea of six, in six apples and applying it to six buses. Six was simply "this amount of that," but even this did not exhaust the content of six. It wasn't until Anna came to grips with shadows that things really got under way. Strange, too, when you consider that a shadow is more or less an absence of something. Anyhow, shadows started a chain reaction, and she took off in every direction at once.

To while away the long winter evenings we had a magic lantern, a fairly large number of funny slides that weren't funny, and about an equal amount of educational slides that weren't educational—unless of course you were interested in the number of square feet of glass in the Crystal Palace or you wanted to know for some reason the number of blocks of stone used in the construction of the Great Pyramid. What was both funny and educational, although I didn't know it at the time, was a lit-up magic lantern with no slides in it. It was funny because when you put your hand in front of the beam, it cast a shadow on the screen, actually a bed sheet. It was educational because it brought forth three extraordinary ideas. Anna's request, "Please can I have the lantern on?" always prompted me to ask, "What do you want to see?" As likely as not her reply would be, "Nuffink, I just want it on." I was more than a little concerned for she would sit there and stare at the rectangle of light. For a long time she would just sit and stare, unmoving. I was torn between breaking this hypnotic trance she seemed to be in and waiting to see what it was all about.

This looking at the rectangle of light went on for about

a week or so. After what seemed to be a lifetime of agony, she spoke, "Fynn, hold a matchbox in the light."

I went forward, matchbox in hand, and held it in the beam of light. The screen filled with the black shadows of hand and matchbox.

After a long and careful scrutiny she exclaimed, "Now a book."

I duly produced a book and held it in the beam. Again this breath-holding look. About a dozen or so various objects were placed in the beam before I was bidden to turn it out. Sitting on the table with the gaslight fully on, I waited for an explanation, but nothing came. My patience cracked wide open and I asked, in as unconcerned a voice as I could manage, "What you cookin' up, Tich?"

Her face pointed in my direction but her eyes were somewhere else.

"It's funny," she murmured. "It's funny."

Sitting there looking at her, I had the queerest feeling that some inner part of her was slowly, so very slowly, turning on its axis. Her eyes were fixed straight ahead, her head turned with painful slowness to the left. Suddenly her concentration broke and she giggled. I was left with the feeling that I had been reading a whodunnit with the last page missing.

This whole episode was repeated six or seven times in as many days; in all other ways she was still her exciting, fun-loving self. For me it was a nail-biting and anxious time. It was on the fifth or maybe sixth repeat that she asked for a sheet of paper and requested that it be pinned onto the screen. This I did. A jug was this day's object and Anna explained that she wanted me to trace around the shadow of the jug with a pencil on the sheet of paper. So there I was, standing with a jug in one hand and a pencil in the other. I couldn't make it; I was about two feet short of the screen. I pointed this fact out to her but she just sat there like some director on a film set, ordering her minions about to achieve the effect she wanted. In response to my plea for help she merely stated, "Stand it on something." I just did what I was told. With the help of a small table and a pile of books I managed to set it up and traced the outline of the jug on to the piece of paper.

"Now cut it out," she commanded.

Feeling that my considerable talents were being wasted on such menial tasks, I told her to do it herself.

"Please," she said, "please, Fynn."

So, with an adequate show of reluctance, I cut it out and handed it to her. With the lantern out and the gas-light on she stared at the cutout, going through the whole rigmarole of screwing her head off in order to—what? Whatever it was seemed to satisfy her, for she nodded, got up, and placed the cutout in the pages of the concordance.

The next night produced three more cutouts, and I was still none the wiser. I didn't know it at the time but Anna had solved her problem. Not a sign, however, hinted at the solution. Anna was marshalling her facts and her ideas. Three days passed before she once again asked for the magic lantern to be put on. Three days of cunningly worded questions. Three days of enigmatic smiles, like some half-pint Mona Lisa. Finally the stage was set.

"Now!" exclaimed Anna with complete confidence. "Now!"

The four cutout figures were taken from the book and placed on the table.

"Fynn, hold this one up for me."

I held the cutout in the beam of the light. What did she want a shadow of a shadow for, I wondered.

"Not that way! Hold it perpendicular to the sheet."

"Rightee are," I replied, holding the paper shadow perpendicular to the sheet.

"Wot you see, Fynn?"

I turned to her. Her eyes were screwed tightly shut; she wasn't looking.

"A straight line."

"Now the next one."

I held the next cutout perpendicular to the screen.

"Wot you see now?"

"A straight line."

The third and fourth also gave straight lines. Natch! Anna had established the fact that any object, be it mountain or mouse, petunia or King George himself, produced a shadow. Now, if we hold this shadow perpendicular to the screen, then all the shadows of all the objects produced a straight line. There was still more to come.

Anna opened her eyes and looked hard at me.

"Fynn, can you hold a line perpendicular to the screen? In your head, I mean. Wot would you see, Fynn? Wot, eh?"

"A spot," I answered.

"Yes." Her smile was brighter than the beam from the magic lantern.

"I still don't get what you're on about."

"That's what a number is."

I suppose the nicest compliment ever paid to me was Anna's silence. That silence I interpreted as, "Well, you've got the intelligence to finish it off yourself, so get to it." I did. Mind you, my mental gymnastics always ended up with, "Do you mean that . . . ?"

It did this time; I started off, "Do you mean to say that . . . ?"

What she meant to say was this: if a number, say seven, could be used to count things as diverse as bank notes and babies, books and bats, then all these diverse things must have something in common. Some common factor, unnoticed and unattended to. What could it be? Things had shadows; having a shadow was a positive indication that something existed. A shadow lost you many of the things that you could not count, like redness and sweetness, and that was good, but it left you with shapes. A shadow had still got too much information attached to it. Since shadows were different, you obviously had to lose some more information. Now since a shadow lost you a lot of useless information, then it was reasonable to suppose that a shadow of a shadow would lose you some more. So it did, if, and only if, you held the shadow perpendicular to the screen, and then all shadows became straight lines. The fact that all these straight lines were of different lengths was something else you didn't want, but the solution to this was easy. Simply make all the straight lines cast shadows and there you are. What all these diverse things had in common, the thing you really counted with, a number, was the shadow of a shadow of a shadow, which was a dot. Every scrap of uncountable information had been lost by this method. This was it. This is what you counted.

Having reduced all the multitude of things to a common essence, the dot, the thing that you really counted, Anna proceeded to unwind things again. With a pencil in one hand, she plonked a dot on a clean sheet of paper.

"Ain't it wonderful, Fynn?" she said, pointing to the dot. "That might be the shadow of a shadow of a shadow of me or a bus or anything; or it might be you."

I had a good look at myself. I didn't recognize myself but I got the point.

She unwound a dot to a straight line, from a line to a shape, from a shape to an object, from an object to a——
Before she knew where she was, she was climbing like a monkey up the tree of higher and higher dimensions. An object, you see, might after all be the shadow of something more complex, and that something might be the shadow of something even more complex, and so on. The mind boggles at the thought. But there was really nothing to it, so I was told. Once you had managed to reduce everything to a dot, you couldn't reduce it any further. That was the end of the line, but as soon as you started to unwind things again, well, where did you stop? There was no reason why you shouldn't go on forever. Except, of course, that there was one thing in this universe that was so complex that it couldn't become any more so. Even I guessed that one. None other than Mister God. Anna had reached the ends of an infinite series of dimensions. At one end of the series was a dot, at the other, Mister God.

Feeding the ducks in the park the next day, I asked her how she had gotten on to the idea of shadows.

"In the Bible," she announced.

"Where in the Bible?"

"Mister God said he would keep the Jews safe under his shadow."

"Oh."

123

"And then St. Peter."

"Wot about St. Peter? Wot he do?"

"Made people better."

"How'd he do that?"

"He put his shadow on ill people."

"Oh! Yes. I should have known."

"An' Old Nick."

"How did he get in?"

"Wot's his name?"

"Satan."

"Another one."

"The devil?"

"No. Another one."

Finally I hit on "Lucifer."

"Yes. Wot's it mean?"

"Light, I think."

"How about Jesus?"

"Yeah, how about Jesus?"

"Wot's he say?"

"Lots of things, I suppose."

"Wot did he call himself?"

"The Good Shepherd?"

"Something else."

"Er—the Way?"

"Something else."

"Oh, you mean the Light?"

"Yes. Old Nick and Jesus—both the Light. You know what Jesus said, don't you? '*I* am the Light.' " She stressed the word *I*.

"What did he say it like that for?"

"So's you won't get muddled."

"How d'you get muddled?"

"Two kinds of light: a pretend one and a real one. Lucifer and Mister God."

Anna's second idea flowed naturally and easily from the first. Shadows were indeed seen to be of the utmost importance in the proper understanding of Mister God and consequently in the proper understanding of Mister God's creation. First we have Mister God and we know that he is Light. Then we have an object and we know this is Mister God's creation. And finally we have the screen on which shadows are formed. The screen is that object that loses us all the redundant information that enables us to do things like sums and geometry and all that.

Now you don't think that Mister God wasted all this miraculous stuff just on simple sums and simple geometry, do you? Oh, no. First of all, you can place the screen at an angle to the beam of light, or you can move the source of light about. The shadows distort, but you can still talk about them in a reasonable way; you can still do sums. Then, of course, you can distort the screen in all sorts of interesting ways, and still you can talk about the shadows in a logical way. Also, you can put the light inside the object and cast the shadow onto a screen, and that is really very interesting. If you make a shadow of a shadow on a screen, then distort the screen, why, a distance like an inch might collapse into nothingness or maybe stretch to I don't know how far. Once you start distorting the screen, well, there's no knowing what kind of sums you might be able to do. That's what Anna called real God stuff. But you can do none of these tricks with a shadow of a shadow of a shadow. That's such a tiny little dot that it won't distort at all, no matter what you do with it.

Anna's final shadow revelation was delivered one wet and windy winter's night—a night that I haven't quite come to terms with in thirty years. I was sitting comfortably and warm by the fire reading. Anna was fiddling about with paper and pencil when it all started.

"Wot you reading, Fynn?"

"All about space and time and stuff like that. You wouldn't be interested."

"Wot's it say?"

"Lots of things about space and time"—and then I made my mistake—"and light."

"Oh!" She stopped writing. "What about light?"

I started to get itchy under the collar; after all, light and shadow were Anna's province.

"Well, a fellow called Einstein has figured out that nothing can go faster than light."

"Oh," said Anna and went on writing. Suddenly she flung over her shoulder, "That's wrong!"

"So it's wrong, is it? Why didn't you stop me?"

The joke misfired.

"Didn't know wot you were reading," she replied.

"All right, then, tell me what goes faster than light."

"Shadows."

"Can't do," I countered, "because the light and the shadow get there at the same time."

"Why?"

"Because it's the light that makes the shadow." I was beginning to get a bit muddled. "Look, a shadow is where there isn't any light. You can't have a shadow getting there before the light does."

She digested this for about five minutes; I had gone back to my book.

"Shadows go faster. I can show you."

"This I've got to see. Start demonstrating."

She hopped off the chair and put on her outdoor coat and macintosh and picked up the large torch.

"Where we off to?"

"Down the cemetery."

"It's pouring with rain and it's perishing dark."

She waved the torch at me, "Can't show you the shadow if'n it's light, can I?"

Outside it was as black as pitch and the rain wasn't waiting to fall down. It was just solid water.

"What are we going to the cemetery for?"

" 'Cos of the long wall."

As the cemetery road led to nowhere in particular, and as the road was bounded on the one side by a railway fence and on the other side by the high cemetery wall, the road wasn't very well lit, and nobody used it very much—I hoped. Reaching the midpoint of the wall, we stopped.

"What now?" I questioned.

"You stand here," and I was stood in the road, about thirty feet from the wall.

"I'm going up there," she continued, "and I'll shine the light on you. You watch your shadow on the wall."

With that explanation she trotted off into the dark. Suddenly the torch light flipped on, fingering about in the darkness until it found me.

"Ready?" came the yell out of the darkness.

"Yes," I yelled back.

"See your shadow?"

"No."

"I'll come nearer. Say when."

The torch bobbed nearer, transfixing me in the middle of the beam.

"Righty ho," I yelled as I made out my dim shadow away down the far end of the wall.

"Now watch your shadow."

She walked a path parallel to the cemetery wall about two feet further away from it than I was. I watched my shadow, staring into the darkness. It zoomed toward me at a fair rate of knots, certainly much faster than Anna was walking. It slowed down as it passed me on the wall and then speeded up again. Anna was walking backward with the light still on me.

Suddenly she was by my side again.

"See it?" she questioned.

"Yeah, I saw it."

"Goes fast, don't it?"

"Sure does. How did you work that one out?"

"The cars. The lights on the cars."

I agreed that my shadow was moving faster than she was walking, but certainly not faster than light, and I said so. I got no answer. By the light of the torch I could see that she was miles away. The outside experiment now finished, she was busy setting up some internal experiment.

I grabbed her hand, saying, "Come on, Tich, let's go to Ma B.'s for a cuppa tea and a bite to eat."

On the way we met Sally.

"You daft?" she said. "What are you doing taking the kid out on a night like this?"

"Not taking," I answered, "being took."

"Oh," said Sally, "one of them?"

"Yes. Come and have a cuppa at Ma B.'s."

"Suits me," replied Sally.

I'd just about finished my pork pie when Anna's internal experiment came to an end.

"The sun," she said, "it's like the lights on the cars."

After a few more moments' thought she stabbed in my direction with her unused fork. "You," she said, "you are like the earth—the wall is—the wall is—squillions of miles away, but it's only a pretend wall." She returned with a bump and noticed Sally for the first time.

"Hello, Sal," she smiled.

"Hi, Tich," replied Sally. "What gives?"

Anna transfixed me with her eyes. "The sun makes a shadow of the earth on the wall—the pretend wall."

"Well," I replied rather doubtfully, "I'm not so sure of that."

"Well it can," she smiled, "in your head it can. If the earth goes round the sun, and the shadow goes on the wall which is——"

"——a squillion miles away." I finished off the question for her.

"How fast," she grinned, "how fast does the shadow go on the wall?" She jabbed her fork into her meat pie and circled it around her head like the earth going around the sun. Her head tilted to one side, and with a big grin she dared me to give an answer.

But I wasn't going to. I wasn't going to say squillions of miles a second, at least not until I had thought about it a bit longer.

I knew I was right, that nothing could go faster than light. I believed it completely. I was certain that Mr. Einstein hadn't missed it.

Looking back over the years, I realize just where I went wrong. Not with the sums, I mean, but with Anna's education. You see, I didn't teach Anna the Right and Proper way to do things. Oh sure, I showed her ways to do things, funny ways, quick ways, hard ways, and all sorts of ways, but not The Right Way. In the first place I wasn't at all sure myself what the Right way was; so naturally Anna had to find out ways for herself. That's what made it all so difficult for me.

EIGHT I suppose that the most frequently used words in Anna's writings and speaking were *Mister God.* Running them a close second were the words that she called the "whuh" words. Whuh words were those words that began with *wh,* and these, so far as Anna was concerned, were question words. *What, which, where, why, who*—all question words—the well-behaved question words. There was, however, a rebel question word; it was *how. How* was undoubtedly a question word, and according to Anna, should have been spelled *whow,* or more exactly *who.* But we'd already got a *who,* so it was obvious to her that somebody must have taken the *w* from the front of the word and simply stuck it on the end. *How* was a more or less well-behaved word; it did at least contain the letters *w* and *h,* which indicated that a question was coming up.

Question words were odd in many ways. Perhaps the strangest thing about a whuh question word was the fact that if you substituted the letter *t* in place of the letter *w* in a question word, you were face to face with an answer word—well, for the most part. Answer words were words that. indicated something; they pointed at something. You didn't point with your finger, you pointed with your tongue. Any word that began with a *th* was a tongue-pointing word. What is a tram? could be answered by That is a tram. Where is the book? is answered by There is the book. *When* and *then* were also a couple of question and answer words. The problems of *which* and *thich, why* and *thy,* and *who* and *tho* were obviously problems that could be cleared up, given a little time. Anna was satisfied that whuh words were, and were meant to be, question words in the same way that *thuh* words, like *that, the, those, there,* etc., were, and were meant to be, answer words.

With regards to language itself, Anna was convinced that it could, by and large, be divided into two parts: the question part of the language and the answer part of the language. Of the two, the question part of the language was the most important. The answer part had a certain satisfaction, but was nowhere near as important as the question part. Questions were a sort of inner itch, an urge to go forward. Questions, that is real questions, had this about them, they were risky things to play about with, but they were exciting. You never quite knew where you were going to land.

This was the problem with places like school and church; they seemed to be more concerned with the answer part of the language than with the question part of the language. The problems that places like school and church raised were absolutely tremendous because of the kind of *answers* they gave you. Certainly you could make up the question from the answer given to you, but the trouble was that so often this kind of question had no real place to land; you just kept on falling forever and ever. No, the mark of a real question was that it landed somewhere. As Anna said, "You can ask the question, Do you like skudding?" It certainly looks like a question, it certainly sounds like a question. "But it don't land no-where." If you supposed that it was a real question, if you supposed that it really landed somewhere, why, you could go on asking questions about it all your life and still get nowhere.

Anna was certain that heaven was, certain that angels and cherubs and things like that were real, and she knew more or less what they were like; at least she knew what they were not like. For one thing, they weren't like those pictures of angels with nice feathery wings. It wasn't the wings that bothered her one bit; it was the fact that they looked like people that bothered Anna. The possibility that an angel could, let alone would want to, blow a trumpet, filled her with the deepest dismay. The idea that, come the resurrection day, Anna would still have the same number of legs, still have eyes and ears, still be generally constructed after the same present pattern, was to her an idea too monstrous to contemplate. Why was it that grownups insisted on talking about where heaven was? The whole question of where heaven was was neither here nor there; it was immaterial; it was nonsense. And why, oh why, were angels and cherubs and things like that, and goodness me, even Mister God himself, represented as human people? Oh no, the question of where heaven was was one of those non-questions, it had nowhere to land, and therefore was no question fit to be asked.

As Anna saw it, the question of heaven was not concerned with *where*, but it was concerned with the perfection of the senses. Language was hard put to it when trying to describe or explain the concept of heaven, but then language depended upon the senses, and it therefore followed that the grasp of heaven was also dependent on the senses. These pictures, these statues, these stories about angels, simply shouted aloud the fact that the perpetrators of these monstrosities had no idea what they were on about. They merely showed quite clearly that angels and suchlike were simply men and women with wings on. They were burdened with the same kind of senses as we were and as such were not fit creatures for heaven. No, whatever the description of heaven was, and that was really most unimportant, it didn't describe a place but the inhabitants. Any place could be heaven where the senses were perfect.

132 Mister God's senses were perfect. Well, it stands to reason, to be able to see us over impossibly immense distances, to hear us, and to know our thoughts were not unreasonable characteristics of Mister God, or for that matter the angels either, but to represent them in stories, paintings, or sculptures with ordinary ears, ordinary eyes, and ordinary shapes was childish in the extreme. If the heavenly hosts had to be painted, then they ought to be represented in such a way as to show the perfection of their senses, and since language depended upon the senses, the perfection of their language too.

The strange insistence of Sunday school Teacher, Miss Haynes, and the Reverend Castle on using the words *seeing* and *knowing* in such a clumsy way was a very sore point with Anna. The Reverend Castle talked about *seeing* Mister God, about meeting him *face to face,* in a sermon one Sunday morning. He never knew how close he was to disaster. Anna grasped my hand tightly, shook her head violently and turned to face me. All her efforts were directed to damping down her inner fires, which would have consumed the Reverend Castle had they been let loose.

When it comes to fires, Old Nick had nothing on Anna. She could make the fires of hell look like glowing embers.

In a whisper that echoed around the church, Anna said, "Wot the 'ell he gonna do if Mister God ain't got no face? Wot'll he do if he ain't got no eyes, wot then, Fynn, eh?"

The Reverend Castle faltered for a second and pressed on, dragging with him the heads and eyes of the congregation.

Anna mouthed the words, "Wot then?"

"Search me," I whispered back.

She pulled at my arm and signaled me to come closer. Her lips plugged into my ear. "Mister God ain't got no face," she hissed.

I turned my face to her, and my raised eyebrows asked the question, How come?

Plugging in again, she said, " 'Cos he don't have to turn round to see everybody, that's why." She settled back in her pew, nodding her head at her own certainty and folded her arms with a full stop.

On our way home from church I asked her what she had meant by "he don't have to turn round."

"Well," she said, "I've got an 'infront' and I've got a 'behind' so I have to turn round to see what's behind me. Mister God don't."

"What's he do then?" I asked.

"Mister God's only got an infront, he ain't got no behind."

"Oh," I nodded, "I see."

The idea of Mister God having no behind struck me as deliciously funny and I tried hard to suppress the giggles. I didn't manage it. I exploded.

Anna was a bit puzzled at my outburst. "Wot you laughing for?" she asked.

"Just the idea of Mister God having no behind," I chortled.

Her eyes narrowed for a moment or two and then she grinned. The grin fanned her eyes into flame and she lit up like a Roman candle. "He ain't got one of them, too!" Her laughter ran along the road, erecting little barricades as it went. The all too obvious and self-satisfied Christian worshipers bumped into the laughter and frowned.

"Mister God ain't got no bum," sang Anna to the tune of "Onward Christian Soldiers."

The frowns turned to scandalized looks of horror. "Disgusting!" said the Sunday Suit, "Little savage!" squeaked the Sunday Boots, "A limb of Satan!" said the Albert Watch dangling from the waistcoat, but Anna went on, laughing with Mister God.

On our homeward journey Anna practiced her newly discovered game with me. In the same manner that she launched her spiritual being at Mister God, so she launched her physical being at me. "Mister God ain't got no bum" wasn't a joke, she wasn't being naughty or just a silly child. It was just an eruption of her spirit. With these remarks she hurled herself at Mister God and he caught her. Anna knew that he would, knew that there was no risk involved. There was really no other way; it just had to be done. This was her way of being saved.

Her game with me was similar. She would stand some distance off, run toward me, and launch herself at me. The run toward me was deliberate and active; the moment after her launch she was completely passive and limp. She made no effort to help me catch her, no effort toward her own safety. Being safe meant not doing these things at all; being saved meant trusting in another.

Being safe was easy. You simply accepted Mister God as a superman who hadn't shaved for about six months or so, that angels looked like men and women with wings on, that cherubs looked like fat little babies with wings that couldn't support a sparrow, let alone twenty-five pounds or more of chubby infant. No, being saved was for Anna only possible in that act of creative violence to the images of being safe.

Every minute of every day Anna lived; she totally accepted her life, and in accepting life, accepted death. Death was a fairly frequent topic of conversation with Anna, never morbid or anxious, simply something that would happen at some time or other, and it was better to have some grasp of it before it happened than to wait until the moment of death and then get panicky about it. For Anna, death was the gateway to possibilities. It was Mum who provided Anna with the solution to the problem of death. Like Anna, Mum had this lovely gift of asking questions that landed somewhere.

"What," she asked us one Sunday afternoon, "was God's greatest creative act?"

Although I didn't go along with Genesis, I answered, "When he created mankind."

I was wrong, according to Mum, so I had another shot. I was still wrong. I ran through the six days of creation and drew nothing but blank looks. There was nothing more that I could think of. It wasn't until I had run out of ideas that I became aware of the exchange between Mum and Anna. So often with Mum that smile happened. It was her Christmas-tree smile, she lit up, she twinkled, and there was no other place to look. She sort of gathered everything around her. Anna was watching her intently, chin cupped in hands. There they sat, looking at each other, Mum with her wonderful smile and Anna with her intense look. The insulation of the six feet or so that separated them was beginning to give way. Anna drilled away at it with her blue eyes while Mum melted it with her smile. Suddenly it happened. Anna slowly placed her hands on the table and pushed herself upright. The gap had been bridged. Anna's matching smile had to wait while astonishment shaped her face. She gasped, "It was the seventh day—course it was—the seventh day."

I looked from one to the other and cleared my throat to capture their attention.

"I don't get it," I said. "God worked all his miracles in six days and then shut down for a bit of a rest. What's so exciting about that?"

136   Anna got off her chair and came and sat on my lap. This I knew. This was her approach to the unseeing and unknowing infant—me.

"Why did Mister God rest on the seventh day?" she began.

"I suppose he was a bit flaked out after six days' hard work," I answered.

"He didn't rest because he was tired, though."

"Oh, didn't he? It makes me tired just to think about it all."

"Course he didn't. He wasn't tired."

"Wasn't he?"

"No, he made rest."

"Oh. He did that, did he?"

"Yes, that's the biggest miracle. Rest is. What do you think it was like before Mister God started on the first day?"

"A perishing big muddle, I guess," I replied.

"Yes, and you can't rest when everything is in a big muddle, can you?"

"I suppose not. So what then?"

"Well, when he started to make all the things, it got a bit less muddly."

"Makes sense," I nodded.

"When he was finished making all the things, Mister God had undone all the muddle. Then you can rest, so that's why rest is the very, very biggest miracle of all. Don't you see?"

Put like that, I did see, and I liked what I saw. It made sense. Sometimes, though, I found that I kicked against being the infant at the bottom of the class, and this feeling often caused me to put a dig in whenever I got the chance.

"I know what he did with all that muddle," I exclaimed, feeling rather pleased with myself.

"Wot?" asked Anna.

"He stuffed it in people's brainboxes."

I had meant it as a bombshell, but it didn't go off;

instead two heads nodded in agreement and pleasure that I had grasped the point so quickly. I did a sharp about-face and accepted their agreeing nods as if I was entirely entitled to them. It left me with a problem. How could I ask the question Why did he stuff the muddle in people's brainboxes? in such a way as not to find myself at the bottom of the class again!

"It's a funny thing, this muddle," I began.

"It ain't," said Anna. "You have to have a muddle in your head before you really know what rest is."

"Oh, yes. Yes. I suppose that must be the reason."

"Being dead is a rest," she went on. "Being dead, you can look back and get it all straight before you go on."

Being dead was nothing to get fussed about. Dying could be a bit of a problem, but not if you had really lived. Dying needed a certain amount of preparation and the only preparation for dying was real living, the kind of preparation old Granny Harding had made during her lifetime. We had sat, Anna and I, holding Granny

Harding's hand when she died. Granny Harding was glad to die; not because life had been too hard for her, but because she had been glad to live. She was glad that rest was near; not because she had been overworked, but because she wanted to order, wanted to arrange, ninety-three years of beautiful living; she wanted to play it all over again. "It's like turning inside out, me dears," she had said. Granny Harding died smiling, died in the middle of a description of Epping Forest on an early summer's morning. She died happily because she had lived happily. Old Granny went to church for the second time in her life.

It was three weeks to the day that we all went to another funeral. About a couple of dozen or more of us went to Skipper's funeral—six or so of the older ones and about twenty or so of assorted sizes. "She won't make old bones," they had said, and they were right. Skipper was a natural practical joker, always ready for a laugh. She would have laughed a lot more but it made her cough and she had been coughing a lot lately. Skipper was just coming up to fifteen when she died. Flaxen-haired, blue-eyed, with skin about as transparent as tissue paper, Skipper funned and punned her way through her fifteen years. Why, it hadn't been all that many weeks ago that we'd all been talking about dying.

It was Bunty who opened the conversation with, "How do you die?"

Someone answered with, "It's easy, you just stop."

Skipper had flipped back with "Sure, it's easy. Dead easy."

We all groaned.

The funeral service was a solemn occasion, far too solemn for such as Skipper. The Reverend Castle went on about the innocence of youth and someone had to stifle a giggle. Lifting his eyes upward, he told us that Skipper was now in heaven. Amen. Little faces all turned upward and little mouths opened wide in appreciation, except for young Dora. She looked downward. She got a good nudge and someone said in one of those thunderclap whispers, "Up—up there."

Dora's head went up to the roof of the church, overbalanced and toppled back with a thud. "I dropped me sweets on the floor," she complained.

The Reverend Castle droned on his easy way, painting his word-picture of Skipper. It wasn't our Skipper he was talking about; at least none of us recognized her. It's a good job that the dead don't talk back. I can just imagine what Skipper would have said, " 'O the bleedin' 'ell he talking about? Silly old sod!" Fortunately the Reverend Castle didn't hear and brought the proceedings to a close. We trooped off to the cemetery to pay our last respects. The kids chucked various items into the grave and walked away. We all stood a few yards off and waited for Buzz. We made tracks for the cemetery gates, passing a twelve-foot angel laying a marble bunch of flowers on a grave.

"D'you reckon Skipper's got wings now?" somebody started up.

"Suppose so," came an answer.

"Don't fancy wings meself."

"Why's that?"

"How can you get yer shirt off?"

"Don't be daft, angels don't have no shirts."

"Wot then?"

"It's a nightie."

"I ain't gonna wear no nightie, it's sissy."

Life had started up again.

"Maggie," someone yelled, "where's 'eaven?"

"Somewheres," replied Maggie.

"It's up there."

"Better not be."

"Why's that?"

"If it was, betcha Skipper'd widdle on yer head."

"Oo, you are 'orrible."

"Buzz, you gonna get married, now Skipper's dead?"

"Silly cow," said Buzz, "what's she wanna die for?"

"Better'n coughing yer guts up for years."

"Suppose so—still."

"Maggie, is there a different heaven for the Protties and the R.C.'s and the Jews and all them?"

"No, only one."

"What's all the different churches and synnigogs for then?"

"I don't know."

"Old Nick done that. Just like Old Nick, he mucks everyfing up."

"D'you reckon Skipper's gone to Old Nick?"

"She'd better not. Old Nick would chuck her out in a couple of days."

"Poor Old Nick. Yer gotta laugh."

"Can't stand that, can Old Nick."

"Stand wot?"

"Laughing. It drives him up the wall."

"What you think Skipper is doing now?"

"Singing hymns, I suppose."

"Don't fancy that lark, singing hymns all the time." This was Mat. Looking upward, he began to yell, and in a moment was joined by all the other kids:

> *Sam, Sam, the dirty old man,*
> *Washed his face in a frying pan,*
> *Combed his hair with a leg of a chair,*
> *Sam, Sam, the dirty old man.*

"Betcha Skipper'll teach all them angels that one."

"Yeah, and 'There was an old man of Lancashire, who——' "

"Not that one, stoopid, it's dirty."

"Cors it ain't. Betcha God laughs."

"Bet he don't."

"Wot's he make us with arses for, if we can't say it?"

"It's dirty, that's all."

"Why's everybody make God out to be miserable for? I wish I was God, I'd laugh."

"Yeah, and what about Jesus?"

"Wot about Jesus?"

"All them pictures make him look like a pansy."

"Bet he didn't look like that."

"His old man was a chippy."

"So was Jesus."

"If'n you sawed up bloody great lumps of wood all day you'd have bloody big muscles."

"Yeah. I bet he was all right."

"Course he was. He had a bloomin' good booze-up an' all."

"Where's it say that?"

"The Bible. He turned the water into wine."

"Good job. My old man can't do that."

"Your old man can't do nuffink."

"Why can't I say 'arse'?"

" 'Cos you can't."

"Jesus had one."

"He didn't say 'arse.' "

"How do you know?"

"Bet he said 'bum.' "

"He didn't, he talked Yiddish."

"You're daft."

"Like that nit at Sunday school, says the rain was the angels crying. Wot the 'ell they got to cry about?"

"Twits like you asking silly questions."

"You reckon God gets fed up?"

"What for?"

"All them prayers and questions."

"If I was God, I'd make people laugh."

"If you was God, you wouldn't have to make 'em."

"If I was God, I'd bash 'em on the head wiv a funderbolt."

"I got a good idea."

"Annuvver miracle!"

"No, straight up. What about starting another church?"

"Stone the perishing crows, ain't we got enough?"

"No. I mean no prayers, and no hymns. We'll all tell funny jokes about Old Nick. That'll make him curl up."

"Yeah, a laughing church."

"Hey, that's good, that is. A laughing church."

And so it went on. Hour after hour, day after day, year after year. Like summer lightning, the conversation flickered and flared, lighting up the dark places, forging a philosophy, a theology, a way of life, something to live with. It was this that Anna was so greedy for. It may not sound like very much, but it was the ore from which the gold came. One thing was certain: Skipper was dead, and as she would have said, "Ah well, that's life!" Being dead was a fact of life. Life hereafter was a fact of being dead.

That night, after Skipper's funeral, I was wakened by a cry of despair from behind the curtains. I went to Anna and I cradled her in my arms. A nightmare was my first thought, or perhaps grief for Skipper. I rocked her gently in my arms and made those kinds of noises that "made it all right again." I was holding her tightly for comfort but she fought her way out of my arms and stood on the bed. I was a bit scared and lost at this turn of events and didn't quite know what to do. I lit the gas. Something seemed to go bad inside me. Anna was standing on the bed, her eyes wild and wide, tears streaming down her cheeks, both hands pressed over her mouth as if to stifle a scream. It seemed as if all the familiar objects in the room suddenly raced away to infinity and the world dissolved into formlessness.

I tried to say something, but nothing came. It was one of those senseless moments; my mind was racing around in circles but my body wasn't in gear. I tried to do something, but my body was frozen. What really frightened me was that Anna didn't see me, I wasn't there for her; I couldn't help her. I cried; I don't know if I cried for her or for myself. Whatever the reason, the miseries took over. Suddenly out of my tear-filled void I heard Anna's voice.

"Please, please, Mister God, teach me how to ask real questions. Oh please, Mister God, help me to ask real questions."

For a moment of eternity I saw Anna as a flame and shuddered as I grasped the uniqueness of being me. How I managed that moment I shall never know, for my strength was not equal to that moment. In some strange and mysterious way I "saw" for the first time.

Suddenly there was a hand on my face, soft and gentle. A hand wiping away my tears and a voice saying, "Fynn, Fynn." The room began to reassemble again; things were once more.

"Fynn, wot you crying for?" asked Anna.

I don't know why, perhaps it was just plain fear, but

I began to swear, coldly and efficiently. Every muscle in my body ached and trembled. Anna's lips were on mine, her arm about my neck.

"Don't swear, Fynn, it's all right, it's all right."

I was trying to make some sort of sense out of that awful and beautiful moment, trying to get back to normality again; it was like climbing down an unending ladder.

Anna was talking again. "I'm glad you came, Fynn," she whispered. "I love you, Fynn."

I wanted to say "Me, too," but nothing happened.

In some curious way I seemed to be facing two ways at once. I wanted to be back among the familiar objects that I knew so well, and at the same time I wanted to experience that moment again. From the middle of my fog of confusion I realized that I was being led back to bed, utterly exhausted. I lay there, trying to make some sense of it all, trying to find some starting point from which I could begin to ask questions. But the words didn't seem to fit together in any reasonable pattern. It was a cup of tea in my hand that started the world turning again.

"Drink it, Fynn, drink it all up."

Anna was sitting on the bed wearing my old blue sweater over her pajamas. She had made the tea, hot and sweet, one for each of us. I heard the scrape of a match on the matchbox and Anna's splutter as she lit a cigarette for me and stuck it between my lips. I got myself up on my elbow.

"What happened, Fynn?" asked Anna.

"God knows," I said. "Were you asleep?"

"Been awake for a long time."

"I thought you were having a nightmare," I muttered.

"No," she smiled, "I was saying my prayers."

"The way you was crying—I thought—"

"That why you cried?"

"I dunno, suppose so. It sort of got kind of empty all of a sudden. It was funny. I thought I was lookin' at myself for a moment. Painful."

She didn't answer for a moment, and then very quietly she said, "Yes, I know."

I was too tired to prop myself up any longer and suddenly I found myself with my head resting on Anna's arm. It didn't seem right, it ought to have been the other way around, but it wasn't and I realized that I liked it, it was what I wanted. We stayed like that for a long time, but there were questions I wanted to ask her.

"Tich," I said, "what were you asking God about real questions for?"

"Oh, it's just sad, that's all."

"What's sad?"

"People is."

"I see. What's sad about people?"

"People ought to get more wise when they grow older. Bossy and Patch do, but people don't."

"Don't you think so?" I asked.

"No. People's boxes get littler and littler."

"Boxes? I don't understand that."

"Questions are in boxes," she explained, "and the answers they get only fit the size of the box."

"That's difficult; go on a bit."

"It's hard to say. It's like—it's like the answers are the same size as the box. It's like them dimensions."

"Oh?"

"If you ask a question in two dimensions, then the answer is in two dimensions too. It's like a box. You can't get out."

"I think I see what you mean."

"The questions get to the edge and then stop. It's like a prison."

"I expect we're all in some sort of prison."

She shook her head. "No, Mister God wouldn't do that."

"I suppose not. What's the answer then?"

"Let Mister God be. He lets us be."

"Don't we?"

"No. We put Mister God into little boxes."

"Surely we don't do that?"

"Yes, all the time. Because we don't really love him. We got to let Mister God be free. That's what love is."

Anna searched for Mister God and her desire was for a better understanding of him. Anna's search for Mister God was serious, but gay; earnest, but lighthearted; reverent, but impudent; and single-minded and multi-tracked. Not that she doubted God's existence for a moment, but it was for some time a sign that he did exist. By the same token, a bus or a flower was also a sign that he existed. How she came by this vision of the pearl of great price I do not know. Certainly it was with her before I met her. It was just my luck that I happened to be with her when she was doing her working out. To listen to her was exhilarating, like flying on one's own; to watch her was to be startled into seeing. Evidence for Mister God? Why, there was nowhere you could look where there wasn't evidence for Mister God; it was everywhere. Everything was evidence of Mister God, and it was at this point that things tended to get out of hand.

The evidence could be arranged in too many ways. People who accepted one sort of arrangement were called by one particular name. Arrange the evidence in a new way and you were called by a different name. Anna reckoned that the number of possible arrangements of the available evidence might easily run into squillions of names. The problem was further complicated by the fact of synagogues, mosques, temples, churches, and all the other different places of worship, and scientific laboratories were not excluded from the list. By any reasonable standards of thinking and behavior nobody could, with their hand on their heart, honestly say that these other people were not worshiping and loving God, even if they did call him by some other name like Truth. She could not and would not say that Ali's God was a lesser kind of God than the Mister God that she knew so well, nor was she able to say that her Mister God was greater or more important than Kathie's God. It didn't make sense to talk about different Gods; that kind of talk inevitably leads to madness. No, for Anna it was all or nothing; there could be only one Mister God. This being so, then the different places of worship, the different kinds of names given to those worshipers could be due to one thing, and to one thing only: the different arrangements of the evidence for Mister God.

Anna solved this problem to her own satisfaction, or better still resolved it, on the piano. I've played the piano for as long as I can remember, but I can't read a note of music. I can listen to music and make a reasonable copy of it by ear, but if I attempt to play the same piece of music by reading the score, I turn it into a dirge. Those little black dots throw me into a flat spin. Whatever I've managed on the piano stems from the popular sheet music of prewar; the little frets with their constellation of dots which showed you how to finger the ukulele—or was it the guitar?—and those cryptic symbols underneath the lines of music such as *Am* 7 or the chord of A minor seventh. This was the kind of music that I learned, limited perhaps, but it did have one great advantage. Given a suitable handful of notes, you could call it a *this* chord or a *that* chord, or perhaps any one of half a dozen names; it all depended on something else.

This, then, was the method I used to teach Anna something about the piano. Soon she was romping through major chords, relative minor chords, minor sevenths, diminished sevenths, and inversions. She knew their names and how to call them. More than that, she knew that the name given to a sprinkling of notes depended on where you were and what you were doing. Of course the question of why a group of notes was called a *chord* had to be gone into. Mr. Weekley's dictionary was called into service. We were informed that *chord* and *accord* were more or less one and the same word. One more flip through the dictionary to find out how the word *accord* was used and we ended up with the word *consent,* and there we stopped.

It wasn't many hours later that day when I was confronted with the open-eyed, open-mouthed look of astonishment on Anna's face. She suddenly stopped playing hopscotch with the rest of the kids and walked slowly toward me.

"Fynn," her voice was a squeak of amazement, "Fynn, we're all playing the same chord."

"I'm not surprised," I said. "What are we talking about?"

"Fynn, it's all them different names for churches."

"So what's that got to do with chords?" I asked.

"We're all playing the same chord to Mister God but with different names."

It was this kind of thing that was so exciting about talking to Anna. She had this capacity for taking a statement of fact in one subject, teasing it until she discovered its pattern, then looking around for a similar pattern in another subject. Anna had a high regard for facts, yet the importance of a fact did not lie in its uniqueness but in its ability to do service in diverse subjects. Had Anna ever been given a convincing argument in favor of atheism, she'd have teased it about until she had got a firm hold of the pattern, viewed it from all sides, and then shown you that the whole argument was a necessary ingredient in the existence of God. The chord of atheism might be a discord, but then discords were in Anna's estimation "thrilly," but definitely, "thrilly."

"Fynn, them names of them chords," she began.

"What about them?" I asked.

"The home note can't be Mister God because then we couldn't call them different names. They would all be the same name," she said.

"I guess you're right at that. What is the home note then?"

"It's me or you or Ali. Fynn, it's everybody. That's why it's all different names. That's why it's all different churches. That's what it is."

It makes sense, doesn't it? We're all playing the same chord but it seems we don't know it. You call your chord a C major while I call the same notes A minor seventh. I call myself a Christian. What do you call yourself? I reckon Mister God must be pretty good at music, he knows all the names of the chords. Perhaps he doesn't mind what you call it, as long as you play it.

NINE Maybe it was the fact that Anna and I had met at night that made the nighttime so magic for us. Perhaps it was because the nighttime could be, and so often was, so surprising. The multitudes of sights and sounds of the daytime got down to manageable size at night. Things and sounds became separate at night; they didn't get muddled up with everything else; and things happened in the dark that couldn't possibly happen in the daylight. It's not impossible to have a conversation with a lamppost at night; do the same thing in the daylight and they would take you off in a padded van.

"The sun is nice," said Anna, "but it lights things up so much that you can't see very far."

I agreed that sometimes the sun was so dazzling that on occasions one was quite blinded. That wasn't what she meant.

"Your soul don't go very far in the daylight 'cos it stops where you can see."

"That supposed to make sense?" I asked.

"The nighttime is better. It stretches your soul right out to the stars. And that," she pronounced, "is a very long way. In the nighttime you don't have to stop going out. It's like your ears. In the daytime it's so noisy you can't hear. In the nighttime you can. The nighttime stretches you."

I wasn't going to argue with that one. The nighttime was the time for stretching, and we often stretched ourselves.

Mum never batted an eyelid over our nighttime rambles. Mum knew that stretching was important, and Mum had been a past master at the art of stretching. Given half a chance she'd have been with us. "Have a nice time," she'd say, "and don't get too lost." She didn't mean in the streets of London Town, she meant up among the stars. You didn't have to explain to Mum about getting lost among the stars. Mum reckoned that getting lost and finding your way were just different sides of the same coin. You couldn't have the one without the other.

Mum was something of a genius, certainly she was a mum in a million. "Why don't you go out," she used to say, "it's raining hard," or, "it's blowing a gale." Whatever mischief the weather was up to, Mum suggested that we go out, just for fun, just to see what it was all about. Outside in the streets windows were being flung open and other mums would be yelling for their various Freds and Berts, Bettys and Sadies to "come in outa that rain! You'll be soaked to the skin." Come storm or tempest, rain or snow, daytime or nighttime, we'd always be encouraged to go out and try it. Mum never protected us from God's works, as she called them. Mum protected us, for a while, from ourselves. She'd light up the big copper so that there was a good supply of hot water when we got home. She did it for years, until she figured we'd got enough sense to do it for ourselves; then she stopped.

Staying out all night was, for Mum, something not to be missed.

Most nighttime people were pretty wonderful people. Most nighttime people liked to talk. Those who thought we were mad or just plain stupid were in the minority. True, there were those who didn't hesitate to tell me exactly what they thought of me. "Fancy taking a child out at a time like this; you must be stark raving mad." "You ought to be home and in bed, you wouldn't get up to any mischief there." The assumption on the part of these people was that the nighttime was for mischief, for foul deeds, for getting up to no good. All God-fearing people went to their beds at night. The night was for the "nasties," for "beasties that go bump in the night," and for Old Nick. Perhaps we were lucky; in all the times that we roamed the streets at night we never ever bumped into a nasty or a beasty, or even Old Nick, only nice people. At first we tried to explain that we wanted to be out, that we liked it, but this only confirmed some people in their suspicion that we were mad, so we gave up any attempt at an explanation and simply went out.

Parting from a little group of nighttime people on one of our walks, Anna remarked, "It's funny, Fynn, ain't it? All the nighttime people have got names."

It was true too. You'd bump into a group of nighttime people round a fire and before you could say "How's your father?" you'd be introduced all round. "That's Lil, she's a bit funny in the 'ead, but she's all right." "That's Old Flintlighter." His real name was Robert Somebody-or-other but everybody called him "Old Flintlighter."

Perhaps it was because the nighttime people had more time to talk to each other, or perhaps they were not over-involved in "making it good." Whatever the reason, the nighttime people talked and talked and shared and shared.

It was on one such night that the bottle was passed. It went from hand to hand round the circle. On each pass, the mouth of the bottle was wiped with a dirty sleeve before a good swig was taken. It was my turn; I did a quick wipe and took a big swig. I wish I hadn't. My inside turned a somersault and everything dried up. Coughing and spluttering, with tears streaming down my eyes, I passed it along to the next man. It tasted like well-seasoned varnish laced with TNT. One mouthful was an experience, two was a punishment, and three was certain slow death.

"That yer first time, cock?" said Old Flintlighter.

"Yes," I gasped, "and me last."

"It gets better as you go on," said Lil.

"What the hell do you call it?" I was getting my breath back.

"That's Red Biddy, that's what it's called," said Old Flintlighter.

"It keeps the cold out when it gets a bit chilly."

"It tastes like petrol to me," I said.

Old Lil cackled. "Ain't that the truth," she said. "Yer gets the taste for it after a bit."

Anna wanted a taste, so I poured a drop on the corner of my handkerchief, half expecting it to burst into flames at any moment. She sucked at the corner of the handkerchief and made a face.

"Ugh," she spat, "it's horrible!"

They all laughed.

It struck me as odd that this ritual of wiping the mouth of the bottle still went on; perhaps it was a leftover from the more palmy days. Certainly no germ could get within a foot of it without curling up.

After that experience we never drank anything else but tea or cocoa. We'd sit on old oil drums or wooden boxes and drink tea from battered old tin mugs, cooking our sausages on the ends of sticks and talking.

Convict Bill, from down under, told of his adventures before the mast. Convict Bill had had so many extraordinary adventures he must have had at least four man-sized adventures per day. What did it matter if they were not true? What did it matter if they were all adventures of the imagination? It was pure genius, pure poetry. It was true. The stars stretched a person out; the stars broke open this prison of a box and let the imagination roam.

Anna, on her oil-drum throne, was always and everywhere the center of attention, her face radiant in the fire's glow as she listened to the adventures of the nighttime people. Her contributions to these occasions varied—a little dance, a song, or a story.

On one such night Anna began a story. Old Flintlighter picked her up and stood her on a packing case. There she stood with the eyes of a couple of dozen nighttime people fixed on her. She told the story of a king who was about to have someone's head chopped off but had a sudden change of heart when he saw the smile of a little child. All the heads nodded in unison and Convict Bill sad, "Ah! It's pretty powerful stuff, a smile is. Why, it reminds me of the time . . ." and he was launched on some new and fantastic adventure.

It was a chilly April night when we first met Old Woody. Old Woody commanded great respect from the nighttime people; obviously well-educated, well-mannered, and utterly content with his life. Old Woody was tall and as straight as a pole. Hawk-nosed, bearded, and with eyes that focused somewhere near infinity. His voice was like roasted chestnuts—warm and brown. When Old Woody smiled it just touched the corners of his mouth. But it wasn't there that you looked for his smile, it was in his eyes. Those eyes just sort of wrapped you up; those eyes were full up with good things; and when he smiled, why, they just poured out all over you.

As we stepped into the light of the fire Old Woody looked up and sized us up for a minute or two. Nobody spoke. His eyes passed from my face to Anna's, and there they stuck. With a smile he held out his hand to Anna and she went across to him and held it. For a long, long moment they stared at each other, showering each other with good things, and smiling fit to bust. They were two of a kind; they didn't need to use language. The exchange was immediate and complete. Standing Anna in front of him, he looked her over once more.

"You're a bit young for this, aren't you, little one?"

Anna held her silence, testing and probing Old Woody. He didn't demand an answer, he wasn't anxious, he was prepared to wait.

He passed the test, so he got his answer. "I'm old enough to live, mister," said Anna quietly.

Old Woody smiled, shifted a wooden box beside him, and patted it. Anna sat down.

I was left standing, so I rummaged around until I found a suitable box to sit on and joined the circle. The silence had been held for three minutes or more. Old Woody was busy stuffing his pipe and testing it to see if it was drawing properly. Satisfied that all was as it should be, he got up, went over to the fire and lit up. He put his hand on Anna's head before he sat down and said something that I couldn't catch. They both laughed. Old Woody took a long and satisfying pull at his pipe.

"Do you like poetry?" he asked.

Anna nodded. Old Woody settled the glowing tobacco in his pipe with his thumb.

"Do you," he said, sucking away, "do you know what poetry is?"

"Yes," replied Anna. "It's sort of like sewing."

"I see," Old Woody nodded, "and what do you mean by sewing?"

Anna juggled the words around in her mind. "Well,

it's making something from different bits that is different from all the bits."

"Um," said Old Woody, "I think that is rather a good definition of poetry."

"Mister," said Anna, "can I ask you a question?"

"Of course," Old Woody nodded.

"Why don't you live in a house?"

Old Woody looked at his pipe and rubbed his thumb on his beard. "I don't think there is a real answer to that question, not put like that. Can you ask it in another way?"

Anna thought for a moment, then said, "Mister, why do you like living in the dark?"

"Living in the dark?" smiled Old Woody. "I can answer that very easily, but can you understand my answer, I wonder?"

"If it's an answer, I can," responded Anna.

"Yes, of course. If it is an answer, you can. That's true, only if it's an answer." He paused, and then, "Do you like the darkness?"

Anna nodded. "It stretches you out big. It makes the box big."

He gave a little chuckle. "Indeed, indeed," he said. "My reason for preferring the darkness is that in the dark you have to describe yourself. In the daylight other people describe you. Do you understand that?"

Anna smiled, and Old Woody reached out a gnarled old hand and gently closed Anna's eyes, held both her hands and settled some inner aspect of himself. This particular little spot in London Town looked by daylight a shambles; at this moment, in the light of the fire, it was pure magic.

Old Woody's firm and strong voice spoke to his God, to Anna, and to all mankind:

In faith, I do not love thee with mine eyes,
For they in thee a thousand errors note;
But 'tis my heart that loves what they despise.

His nut-brown chuckle broke the spell. "Do you know that one? It's one of Shakespeare's sonnets. They," he said, and his arms swept out to embrace the world, "will tell you and encourage you to develop your brain and your five senses. But that's only the half of it, that's only being half a human. The other half is to develop the heart and the wits." He ticked them off on one old gnarled hand with the end of his pipe. "There's common wit, there's imagination, there's fantasy, there's estimation, and there's memory." Old Woody's face turned upward, his spirit danced and was warmed out among the stars, while his body remained with us and was warmed by the old tin-can brazier. "Never let anyone rob you of your right to be complete. The daylight is for the brain and the senses, the darkness is for the heart and the wits. Never, never be afraid. Your brain may fail you one day, but your heart won't." He returned like a comet, leaving behind a shining trail of love.

He stood up and stretched himself, looked around at all the faces, and his gaze stopped at Anna. "I know you, young lady, I know you well." He pulled his coat closer round his old shoulders, moved out of the circle of light, and stopped and smiled once more at Anna. He held out his arm to her and spoke:

Thus doth she, when from individual states
She doth abstract the universal kinds,
Which then reclothed in divers names and fates,
Steal access thro' our senses to our minds.

Then he was gone. No, not gone, for some part of him, perhaps the biggest part of him, remained and remains even to this day. We stayed looking into the fire for ten minutes or so. We asked no questions, for there were no answers. We didn't even say good-bye to the night people as we left. I wondered if we had left as much behind us at our going.

We walked on slowly through the streets of London, each afloat on our own thoughts. One of the council's motorized road sweepers made clean the mess of the day. It came toward us, spraying the roadway and the pavement as it came, its large cylindrical brushes clearing up the streets of London for the daylight people. We did a *pas de deux* to the right as its spray hissed onto the pavement and one to the left as it passed us.

Anna switched on her klaxon-horn laugh and spun like a top with joy. Pointing after the receding sweeper, she said. "Fairies; they're like fairies."

"Some fairies," I chuckled.

"Like what you read to me—about Puck."

The mood and joy of the night caught hold of me. I ran and leapt on to a nearby pillar box and stood up and declaimed the lines of Puck to the night:

> *I am sent with broom before,*
> *To sweep the dust behind the door.*

Titania pirouetted and circled the pillar box in fairy dance. A policeman advanced in the distance, and pointing a finger at him, I yelled, "How now, spirit! Whither wander you?" His What do you think you're up to? was almost lost in our laughter. I jumped off the pillar box and grabbed Anna by the hand and we raced after the disappearing road sweeper. We dashed through its fountains of spray and waited ahead of it, breathless with running and laughter.

"Look! It's Moth and Mustardseed," I gasped out.

"No, it's not; it's Peaseblossom and Cobweb," she squeaked.

Our feet and legs were drenched as the sweeper passed. It went on for a few more yards and then stopped; the spray was turned off. The cab door opened and Mustardseed stepped to the ground. The sight of a six-foot, 250-pound, overall-clad Mustardseed was too much; we clung to each other, helpless with laughter. Mustardseed moved toward us from one direction while the policeman, with measured tread, approached from behind us. We fled howling down a side street and stopped at some safe distance. The policeman and Mustardseed, now joined by Moth, were looking down the street after us. What they were talking about, who knows? but my guess was that it was something to do with the madness of the young. I grabbed Anna's hand again and we ran. We didn't stop running until we came to the embankment. We climbed onto the parapet and opened our sandwiches and munched them while we watched the night traffic on the Thames pass by.

After finishing the sandwiches I lit a cigarette. Anna climbed down and began a lonely game of hopscotch on the pavement. She got about thirty yards away, turned, ran back, and stood in front of me.

"Hello, Fynn." She twirled around and parachuted her skirt.

"Hello, Anna." I inclined my head and threw out a

gracious hand.

She was off again, hopping away for all she was worth, chanting a one-two-three song. She stopped and performed a little dance of pure joy. She ran back, her finger drawing a wavy line on the wall. She stopped again about five yards short of me, turned again, and drew another wavy line with the fingers of her other hand on the wall.

Twenty or thirty times she covered that twenty-yard length of wall. Long and slow waves, short and fast waves. Sometimes she walked as she drew her wavy lines, sometimes she went backward and then forward as fast as her legs would carry her. The wall showed no signs of her activity, bore no witness to her thoughts; it remained a blank, but then Anna was writing on her inner blackboard.

At the end of her run she stopped, the lamplight glinting on her hair. She shook her head violently and a cloud of copper sparks rose up and settled. She began to walk, head down, heel to toe along the cracks of the paving stones, her course unplanned and uncharted, led only by the chance intersection of the paving-stone cracks. I doubt if she was even aware of what she was doing. This activity absorbed about one percent of her attention. The other ninety-nine percent had got turned around and was looking inside at something. It's funny how you learn to read the signs. This was the impending revelation prelude, that is, if it got worked out. I put my packet of cigarettes and matches beside me. It was possible I wouldn't have another chance for an hour or so, if I had read the signs right.

Her walk finished, she drifted over to the wall, leaned against it, and remained perfectly still for a minute or two. With about as much attention as she had walked the cracks of the pavement, she shuffled her feet forward about a yard or so. She made an angle with the wall, supported only by her heels and the back of her head. I nearly yelled, but I didn't. It wouldn't have made much difference if I had; there wasn't much of her outside. She couldn't have heard me where she was.

She didn't walk back, she didn't hop, jump, skip, or run back, she rolled back. For thirty or more yards she rolled, balanced between head and heels. Over and over and over she rolled, ending up with her head buried on my legs, and there she stayed.

Her voice, muffled by my trousers, said, "I'm dizzy."

"Ain't that the truth," I replied.

"The wall's hard," came her muffled voice.

"So's your head."

I got a sharp don't-be-funny bite on my leg.

"Oi! that hurts," I reminded her.

"So does my head."

"It's your own fault. You shouldn't be so daft. What was all that for?"

"I was thinking."

"That was thinking?" I asked. "Please God I never learn to think."

"Do you want to know what I was thinking about, Fynn?"

She looked up at me.

"If I've got a choice," I answered, "no, I don't."

She knew that I was teasing her and her smile told me that I didn't have a choice anyway.

"It can't be light." Anna gave that sentence a finality that was irrefutable.

"So, fine," I said. "If it can't be light, what is it?"

"Mister God can't be light." The words flew like stone chippings as Anna hacked away with her mental chisels.

I could imagine Mister God edging forward on his

golden throne and peering down through the clouds, a little anxious to know what kind of a mold he was being forced into now. I had the itch to look upward and say, "Relax, Mister God. Just relax, you're in safe hands." I reckon Mister God must get a bit fed up now and again considering all the various shapes we'd pressed on him over the last umpteen thousand years, and I don't suppose we've come to the end of it yet, not by a long chalk.

"He can't be light, can he? Can he, Fynn?"

"Search me, Tich. Search me."

"Well he can't be, 'cos what about them little waves we can't see and the big waves we can't see? What about them?"

"See what you mean. I reckon things would look a whole lot different if we could see by those waves."

"I think that the light's inside us. That's what I think."

"Could be. Could be you're right," I said.

"I think it's so's we can *see* how to see," she nodded her head, "that's what I think."

Upstairs Mister God—if you'll pardon the image—slapped his leg and turned to his angel hosts and said, "How about that! How about it?"

"Yes," continued Anna, "the Mister God light inside us is so's we can see the Mister God light outside us, and—and, Fynn," she jumped up and down with excitement as she rounded it all off, "the Mister God light outside us is so's we can see the Mister God light inside us."

She played the whole melody over again to herself in silence. With a grin that would have put the Cheshire cat to shame, she said, "That's nice, Fynn. Ain't it nice?"

I agreed that it was nice, very nice, but I was beginning to think that I had had just about enough for one night. I was glutted and needed a little time to digest the night's happenings, but not Anna; she had just got into her stride.

"Fynn, can I have the chalks?"

It was time to come up for air and I rummaged about in my pockets for the tin.

Going out with Anna fell naturally into three categories. There was "oozing" along, like we were doing this night. The demands of oozing were simply met. Two smallish tins containing colored chalks, string, bits of colored wool, 'lastic bands, a small bottle or two, paper, pencil, pins, and a few other knickknacks, odds and ends, and suchlike.

Category two was going for a walk. This was a bit more complicated. Over and above the two tins just for oozing, going for a walk demanded such things as collapsible fishing net, jam jars, boxes of various sizes, tins, bags, etc., etc. Ideally we should have had a five-ton truck following us, carrying everything necessary for going for a walk. If Mother Nature had been a little kinder to all the bugs, beetles, caterpillars, frog spawn, and what-have-you that Anna brought back from going for a walk, I reckon that London would have ground to a halt. We'd have been up to our eyes in frogs and bugs.

The last category was going for a walk with a fixed purpose in mind. This was a daunting experience, such as would give you nightmares for the rest of your life. To satisfy every contingency in going for a walk with a fixed purpose in mind would take about three—better make it half a dozen—vans. Little items, like maybe an oil rig or two, air compressors, a hundred-foot ladder, a diving bell, a crane or two; little things like that. It's far too painful to talk about. After the three times we went for a walk with a fixed purpose in mind I couldn't stand upright for a week.

Carrying chalks about, then, came as naturally as breathing. They went everywhere with me. Carrying about these chalks produced a sort of Walter Mittyish fantasy game. I'd be at the opera, or maybe the proms, and the performance would stop. Someone would step forward and say, "Has any gentleman in the audience got a piece of chalk?" I'd get up and say, "Yes, I've got some. What color would you like?" Applause! Applause! Nobody ever asked me, except Anna that is, but Anna never used the chalks as a prop for fantasy; she used them to explain the fantastic.

I passed her the chalks. She knelt down on the pavement and drew a large red circle.

"Pretend that's me," she said.

Outside the circle she liberally sprinkled a number of dots. About the same number of dots were sprinkled inside the circle. She beckoned me off my perch on the wall. I went and knelt beside her. Looking around, she pointed to a tree.

"That," she said, "is that there," and she pointed to a dot outside the circle and marked it with a cross. Then, pointing to a dot inside the circle, she said, "That is that dot outside the circle, and that is the tree," and with her finger on the tree dot inside the circle, she continued with, "And that's the tree inside me."

"I seem to have been here before," I murmured.

"And that," she exclaimed in triumph, laying her finger on a dot inside the circle, "is a—is a—a flying elephant. But where is it outside? Where is it, Fynn?"

"There ain't no such beastie, so it can't be outside," I explained.

"Well then, how did it get into my head?" She sat back on her heels and stared at me.

"How anything gets into your head beats me, but a flying elephant is pure imagination, it's not factual."

"Ain't my imagination a fact, Fynn?" she quizzed me with a tilt of her head.

"Sure, of course your imagination is a fact, but what comes out of it isn't necessarily a fact." I was beginning to wriggle a bit.

"Well then, how did it get in there"—she thumped the inside of the circle—"if it ain't out there?" she went on with a few more thumps. "Where did it come from?"

I was thankful that I wasn't given the opportunity to answer that one. She was in full flight. She got up and walked around the diagram of her universe.

"There's a lot of things out there that ain't in here."

She leaped from the edge of the universe into the circle of herself and knelt down.

"Fynn, did you like my painting?"

"I liked it fine," I said. "I thought it was pretty darn good."

"Where," she said with her hands on her hips, "was it?"

I pointed to a dot outside the circle. "There, I suppose."

She scrabbled backward until she was clear of the diagram and pointed a finger to the center of the circle. Her finger stabbed out her sentence. "There, that's where I painted it—inside me."

She remained silent for a long moment, then, sweeping her hands over the diagram, she said in a puzzled voice, "Sometimes I don't know if I am locked out or locked in."

Touching the inner dots and then the outer dots, she

continued, "It's funny, sometimes you look inside and find something outside and sometimes you look outside and find something inside. It's very funny."

As we knelt considering the southeast sector of Anna's universe, a pair of shining size-twelve boots appeared in the northwest sector and a voice said, "Well, well, if it isn't Master Puck and the Lady Titania."

"Blimey, it's Oberon," I muttered, looking up and seeing the policeman.

"Haven't you got a home to go to? And what do you think you're up to, drawing pictures on the pavement?"

"We've got a home to go to," I admitted.

"That ain't a picture, mister," said Anna, still hunkered down on the pavement.

"What's it supposed to be then?" asked the policeman.

"It's really Mister God. That's me, that's inside me and that's outside me, but it's all Mister God."

"Well now," said the policeman, "it's still drawing on the pavement, and that's not allowed."

Anna reached out and pushed a pair of size twelves out of her universe. The policeman looked down at Anna.

"You've just flattened a couple of billion stars," I told him.

The policeman may have represented law and order but Anna was concerned with higher laws and higher orders.

"That's you, mister," Anna was undeterred and went on, "and that's you inside me. Ain't it, Fynn?"

"Sure. Sure is, constable, that's you right enough," I agreed.

"Only you don't look like that really. You look like this." She shuffled a few feet to one side and drew another large circle and filled it with dots. 167

"That's me inside you," she said, pointing to a dot, "but that dot is really that circle. That's me."

The policeman was leaning forward looking at Anna's universe. "Ah!" he said knowingly. He looked at me and raised his eyebrows. I shrugged my shoulders. After a hum or two he pointed his size twelves at one of the outside dots.

"Know what that is, Titania?"

"Wot?" said Anna.

"That's the Sarge. He'll be along in a few minutes and if this pavement isn't cleaned by then, you'll be in one of these." His foot described a large circle. "Know what that is? That's a police station." His broad smile softened his gruff voice.

Anna took my offered handkerchief and erased the universe from the pavements of Westminster embankment. Standing up, she flapped the chalk dust from my handkerchief and handed it to me.

"Mister," she said, "do you always work here?"

"Most times," the policeman replied.

"Mister," Anna took his hand and pulled him to the wall, "mister, is the Thames the water, or the hole it goes in?"

The policeman looked at her for a moment and then replied, "The water, of course. You don't have a river without water."

"Oh," said Anna, "that's funny, that is, 'cos when it rains it ain't the Thames but when it runs into the hole it is the Thames. Why is that, mister? Why?"

The policeman looked at me. "Is she having me on?"

"You're being let off lightly," I said. "I get it all day long."

The policeman had had enough. "Hop it, you two, hop it or I'll—Oh yes. One last word of warning. You'd better go home that way," he pointed with his finger. "Er —Peaseblossom and Cobweb," his grin was difficult to control, "will be along here in no time. If you're still around, you might get your Bottom smacked—Get it?" he chuckled, pleased with himself.

"Comics," I muttered, "the whole world's full of comics."

I grabbed Anna's hand and led her away. "Nice work, Tich, nice work. A good bit of thinking, all that Thames stuff."

"Oh," murmured Anna, "but when do you, Fynn? When do you start calling it the Thames and when do you stop calling it the Thames? Do you have a mark? Do you, Fynn?"

Old Woody was right. The daylight schooled the senses and the nighttime developed the wits, stretched the imagination, sharpened fantasy, hammered home the memory and altered the whole scale of values.

I began to realize why most people went to sleep in the nighttime—it was easier. A whole lot easier.

TEN

It looked pretty certain that the war would come. Already the gas masks were making rude noises in the streets. The men with the Anderson shelters were dumping corrugated iron sheets in back gardens. Notices about gas attacks, sirens, shelters, and what to do "if," were multiplying like the spots of some disease. The decay of war was spreading everywhere. The walls against which the kids played their ball games had become the notice boards of war. The rules of "four sticks" chalked up on the wall had been covered over with the regulations for the blackout. We were being instructed in the rules of a new game. On very rare occasions an instruction said something other than had been intended: ALL EXPECTANT MOTHERS MUST SHOW THEIR PINK FORMS. It would have been nice to think that it had been done deliberately, but it hadn't.

The infection of war was spreading through the kids. Balls were no longer things to bounce; balls had become bombs. Cricket bats were pressed into service as machine guns. Kids with outstretched arms gyrated through imaginary skies with a *rat-a-tat-tat,* shooting down enemy planes or shooting up enemy soldiers. A shriek of *wheeeeee, booooom* and a dozen kids died in feigned agony. "Bang, you're dead!"

Anna held tightly to my hand and pressed herself close to me. It wasn't the kind of game that she could play; the acting and the pretending belonged to something real, and it was this reality that Anna saw so clearly. She pulled at my hand and we went indoors and out into the garden. It wasn't much better there, for over the housetops a barrage balloon made mock of the skies. She turned a full circle looking at these intruders in the sky. She looked me full in the face as her hand stretched out for mine. A frown flickered over her face.

"Why, Fynn? Why?" she asked, searching my face for an answer.

I could give her no answers. Kneeling down, she gently touched the few wild flowers that grew in the backyard. Bossy arrived and rubbed his battered old head on her leg. Patch, lying full length, eyed her with concern. It must have been the best part of an hour that I stood there watching her touch and explore these few square yards of garden. Delicately and reverently her fingers moved from beetle to flower, from pebble to caterpillar. I was waiting for her to cry, expecting her at any moment to run to my arms, but she didn't. I wasn't at all sure what was going on in her mind. All I knew was that the hurt was deep, perhaps too deep for my comfort.

Some time ago I had started to light up a cigarette, but I hadn't got very far. It was still unlit between my lips when I heard her say, so very quietly, "I'm sorry." She wasn't talking to me, she wasn't talking to Mister God. She was talking to the flowers, to the earth, to Bossy and to Patch and to the little bugs and beetles. Humanity asking the rest of the world for forgiveness.

I was intruding here so I went into the kitchen and swore. It struck me as curious that since knowing Anna I was swearing much more frequently. It ought to have been the other way around, but it wasn't. I grabbed the unlit cigarette out of my mouth. It had stuck to my lips and it felt as if I had pulled half the skin from my lips. It made me swear some more, but it didn't make me feel any better.

I don't know how long I sat there. It seemed forever. It was the horror of my own imagination that drove me into the garden again. My imagination had somehow provided me with a machine gun and I was busy killing off those who had caused Anna so much hurt. Confused and

171

bewildered at my own violent thoughts, I went out into the backyard half afraid that in some mysterious way she had divined them.

She was sitting on the garden wall with Bossy on her lap. She grinned as I approached her, not one of those full-blooded grins, but full enough for me to slam the door on my own violence.

I went back into the kitchen and put on the kettle. Soon we were both sitting on the wall drinking our cocoa. My mind was racing away with questions I wanted to ask but I managed not to. I wanted to be assured that she was all right, but I wasn't given that assurance. I knew that she wasn't all right. I knew that the horror of the impending war had struck deep down inside her. No, she wasn't all right, but she was managing very well. For Anna, this war creeping up on us was a deep sorrow of the soul. It was me that was anxious.

Later that evening, when Anna was ready for bed, I suggested she could come into bed with me if she wanted to, to give her comfort, to give her protection, of course. Lord, how easy it is to fool yourself, how easy to cover up your own maggots of fear, by pretending they belong to someone else. I knew full well that I was concerned for her, that I was aware of her distress, and that I was ready to do anything to comfort her. It was only in the middle of the night that I realized how much I needed her assurance that she was all right, how much her sheer sanity protected me. For all her few years, I saw her then as I see her now, the sanest, the most uncluttered, and the most direct of beings. Her ability to ignore the excesses of information, dismiss the useless frill, and uncover the heart of things was truly magical.

172

"Fynn, I love you." When Anna said that, every word was shattered by the fullness of meaning she packed into it. Her *I* was a totality. Whatever this *I* was for Anna was packed tight with being. Like the light that didn't fray, Anna's *I* didn't fray either; it was pure and all of one piece. Her use of the word *love* was not sentimental or mushy; it was impelling and full of courage and encouragement. For Anna, *love* meant the recognition of perfectibility in another. Anna *saw* a person in every part. Anna *saw* a *you.* Now that is something to experience, to be seen as a *you,* clearly and definitely, with no parts hidden. Wonderful and frightening. I'd always understood that it was Mister God who saw you so clearly and in your entirety, but then all Anna's efforts were directed to being like Mister God, so perhaps the trick is catching if only you try hard enough.

By and large, I thought I could understand Anna's attitude to Mister God, but on one aspect I got stuck completely. Perhaps it was hidden in "Thou didst hide these things from the wise and understanding and didst reveal them unto babes." How she managed it, I truly don't know, but in some manner she had scaled the walls of God's majesty, his awe-inspiring nature, and was on the other side. Mister God was a "sweetie." Mister God was fun, Mister God was lovable. Mister God was for Anna pretty straightforward, not presenting her with any real problem in the understanding of his nature. The fact that he could, and often did, put a large monkey wrench in the works was neither here nor there. He was perfectly free to do so, and obviously it was for some good purpose, even though we were not able to see or understand that purpose.

Anna saw, recognized, admitted to, and submitted to, all those attributes of God so often discussed. Mister God was the author of all things, the creator of all things, omnipotent, omniscient, and at the very heart of all things—except. . . . It was this exception that Anna saw as the key to the whole thing. This exception was funny, exciting, and made Mister God the sweetie he was.

What puzzled Anna was that nobody had seen it before —at least, if they had seen it, nobody seemed willing to talk about it. It was very odd, since it was for Anna so strange a thing that only Mister God could have thought about it. All the other qualities of Mister God, those qualities so often talked about in church and school, were magnificent, tremendous and, let's face it, a little frightening. Then he had gone and done this thing. It made him lovable, funny, giggly.

You could, if you wished, deny that Mister God existed, but then any denial didn't alter the fact that Mister God was. No, Mister God was; he *was* the kingpin, the center, the very heart of things; and this is where it got funny. You see, we had to recognize that he was all these things, and that meant that we were at our own center, not God. God is our center, and yet it is we who acknowledge that he is the center. That makes us somehow internal to Mister God. This is the curious nature of Mister God: that even while he is at the center of all things, he waits outside us and knocks to come in. It is we who open the door. Mister God doesn't break it down and come in; no, he knocks and waits.

Now it takes a real super kind of God to work that one out, but that's just what he's done. As Anna said, "That's very funny, that is. It makes me very important, don't it? Fancy Mister God taking second place!" Anna never got involved in the problem of free will. I suppose she was too young, but she had got to the heart of the matter: Mister God took second place, ain't that something!

It was after ten o'clock on a Sunday morning. Anna had been up for a long time. She was shaking me awake with one hand and holding a cup of tea with the other. My one opened eye registered on the teetering cup and saucer in her left hand. It was more than possible that the cup would end up in bed with me if she shook much harder. I moved across the bed to give myself more room for any emergency maneuver.

"Desist, infant," I implored.

"Cuppa tea, Fynn," she plonked down on the bed. The cup gave a last frantic twirl around the saucer and settled down. After scraping the bottom of the cup on the saucer edge she handed it to me. The amount of tea left at the bottom of the cup might have been enough to drown a fly or two, or at least certainly inconvenience them. I lifted the cup to drain what was there and was smitten on the nose by half a dozen lumps of undissolved sugar. I made a face at her.

"That is tea?" I questioned.

"Drink wot's in the saucer then. I'll hold it for you."

I'm never at my best first thing in the morning and need both my arms to prop myself up. I sat on the edge of the bed and braced myself, closed my eyes and opened my mouth. The saucer rattled against my back teeth as she thrust it in and tipped it up. I got about a third of the tea inside me and the rest outside. Anna giggled.

"A drink I need; a wash I can wait for. Away to the kitchen and start brewing."

I pointed to the door. She went.

"Fynn's awake," she yelled. "He wants some more tea. He spilt that lot down his pajamas."

"May you be forgiven," I muttered as I took off my pajama jacket and mopped my chest with the dry bit.

You didn't have to wait long for tea in our house. Tea was for us what serum is for a casualty ward—ever present. Tea with saffron was good for something or other

175

—fevers, I believe. Tea with peppermint was good for flatulence. Tea woke you up and tea sent you to sleep. Tea without sugar was refreshing, tea with sugar was energizing, tea with a lot of sugar was good for shock. For me, waking up was a shock, so the first cup of tea of the day was nice and sweet.

Anna arrived back in a couple of shakes with more tea.

"Will you make me two paddle wheels this morning?" she asked.

"Could be," I answered. "Where you paddling off to?"

"Nowhere. I want to do an experiment," she replied.

"What size paddle wheels and what are they for?" I questioned.

"Little ones like this," and her hands measured about three inches apart. "And it's for finding out about Mister God."

Requests like that I took in my stride these days. After all, if it was possible to read sermons in stones and things, why not in paddle wheels?

"And can I have the big bath, and some hose pipe, and a tin with a hole in it? I might want something else but I don't know yet."

While I made the paddle wheels Anna assembled her experiment. The paddle wheels were mounted on axles. A large cylindrical tin had a half-inch hole drilled in its side near the bottom of the tin. One of the paddle wheels was soldered inside the tin across the newly drilled hole. After about an hour of hectic activity I was called into the yard to see the Mister God experiment in action.

A hose from the tap was filling the large bath. The tin with its paddle wheel sat in the middle of the bath, weighted down with stones. As the water poured in through the hole, the paddle wheel was turning. More hose pipe was doing service as a syphon, taking the water out of the tin, falling onto and spinning the second paddle wheel, and ending up going down the drain. I walked around the experiment and raised my eyebrows.

"Do you like it, Fynn?" asked Anna.

"I like it. But what is it?" I asked.

"That's you," she said, pointing to the tin with its paddle wheel.

"Bound to be. What am I doing?"

"The water is Mister God."

"Gotcha."

"The water comes out of the tap into the bath."

"I'm still with you."

"It goes into the tin, that's you, through the hole, and makes you work," she said, pointing to the spinning wheel, "like a heart."

"Ah!"

"When you work, it comes out of this tube," she pointed to the syphon, "and that makes the other wheel work."

"What about the drain?"

"Well," she hesitated, "if I had a little pump like Mister God's heart I could pump it all back into the bath. Then I wouldn't need the tap. It would just go round and round."

So there you are then. How to make a model of Mister God, with a couple of paddle wheels. No home should be without one. I sat on the wall and smoked a cigarette while I watched Mister God and me spinning paddle wheels.

"Ain't it good, Fynn?"

"Sure is good. We'd better take it to church on Sunday. It might give somebody some ideas."

"Oh no, we couldn't do that. That would be bad."

"How's that?" I asked.

"Well, it isn't Mister God, but it's a little bit like him."

"So what? If it works for you and it works for me, that's fine. It might work for someone else."

"It works because me and you is full up."

"And what might that mean?"

"Well, if you are full up, you can use anything to see Mister God. You can't if you're not full up."

"Why's that? Give me a for-instance."

She never hesitated.

"The cross! If you're full up, you don't need it 'cos the cross is inside you. If you're not full up, you have the cross outside you and then you make it a magic thing."

She tugged at my arm and our eyes met. She spoke quietly and slowly. "If you're not full up inside you, then you can make anything a magic thing, and then it becomes an outside bit of you."

"Is it that bad?"

She nodded. "If you do that, then you can't do what Mister God wants you to do."

"Oh! What's he want me to do then?"

"Love everybody like you love yourself, and you've got to be full up with you to love yourself properly first."

"Like most of a person is outside," I said.

She smiled. "Fynn, there ain't no different churches in heaven 'cos everybody in heaven is inside themselves."

Then she went on, "It's the outside bits that make all the different churches and synagogues and temples and things like that. Fynn, Mister God said 'I am,' and that's what he wants us all to say—that's the hard bit."

My head went up and down in bewildered agreement.

178   "I am . . . that's the hard bit. I am." Really get around to saying that and you're home; really mean it and you're full up—you're all inside. You don't have to want

things outside you to fill up the gaps inside you. You don't leave bits of you hanging around on objects in shop windows, in catalogs or on advertising hoardings. Wherever you go you take your whole self with you; you don't leave bits lying around to get stamped on; you're all of a piece; you're what Mister God wants you to be. And "I am," like he is. Hell's bells! All this time I had thought that going to church was in order to look for God, for praising him. It didn't dawn on me what Mister God was doing. All this time he had been working overtime trying to knock a bit of sense into my noddle, trying to turn an "It is" into an "I am." I got the message. That was the Sunday I really signed on.

I was beginning to get the hang of this "I am" stuff. Considering how important it was to Mister God, I was finding it not too impossible to cope with. The tricky bit was looking inside yourself to see what bits of the works were missing. Once you'd overcome that hurdle, the rest was fairly simple. My first real peek inside myself caused me to slam the door in a hurry. "That's me in there!" Holy cow, I looked more like an overgrown Gruyère cheese—full of holes. Anna's remark that You're full up, Fynn, I now saw as an encouraging statement rather than a factual one.

After getting over the shock, I opened the door a crack and took another peek. It wasn't long before I was able to identify one of the holes. It was shaped like a motorbike. What's more, I recognized that hole. It was an exact fit of the motorbike in the shop window down the High Street.

After some practice it became more and more easy to identify the holes: a rather super microscope; one of these newfangled television things; and a clock that told you the time in Bombay, Moscow, New York, London, and a few other places, all at the same time. There were bits of me all over the place, leaving identical holes inside me. I was, to say the least, spread out a bit. Somewhere down the line it had all gone wrong. I was certain that I hadn't started out with these holes. It was those damned banners that kept on cropping up: GET ON, GET AHEAD, A MOTORBIKE MAKES YOU SOMEONE, A CAR IS EVEN BETTER, TWO CARS, AND, BROTHER, YOU'VE HIT THE JACKPOT. I had fallen for it, hook, line and sinker. The banners were inside me and they were rooted in pretty fertile soil. The more banners inside me, the more bits of me were outside me. "Most of a person is outside." You can say that again.

There was no overnight miracle, no sudden flash of revelation. It crept up on me unannounced, and I'm still trying to work on it. Like a child learning a new word, I found myself struggling with "I want to be me," "I do want, I really do want to be *me*." It wasn't so difficult to open the doors these days. I now knew where I was. The motorbike hole was still there, but it seemed to be flickering a bit, like some faulty electric light bulb. Then one day it went out. The hole was no longer there, a good-sized bit of me had come home. I was on my way at last. A couple of peeks inside me and I realized that I was beginning to fill up. The world was an all right place in spite of the war.

ELEVEN It was a beautiful sunny day. The street was full of kid noises. Laughter drowned the sounds of marching feet, when suddenly the world fell to pieces.

One scream killed the laughter. It was Jackie's. I turned around in time to catch her in my arms as she hurled herself at me. Her face was a white mask of horror.

"Fynn! Oh Christ! It's Anna. She's dead! She's dead!"

Her scarlet fingernails dug into my chest and the ice-cold water of fear flooded over me. I ran down the street. Anna was lying across the railings, her fingers clinging to the top of a wall. I lifted her off and cradled her in my arms. A flicker of pain narrowed her eyes.

"I slipped outa the tree," she murmured.

"All right, Tich, hold on. I've got you."

Suddenly I felt terribly sick. Out of the corner of my eyes I had seen something, something that in a curiously distorted way was even more terrifying than this injured child in my arms. Her fall had broken off the top part of one of the railings. A broken iron stump. A few years ago nobody could see that, now it was clear for all to see. This iron stump, these crystal mountains, were now red with shame and horror at its part in this dreadful thing.

I carried Anna home and put her to bed. The doctor came and dressed her wounds and left me with her. I held her hands and searched her face. The pain flickered across her eyes but was chased away by a grin that slowly blossomed over her face. The grin won; the pain was hidden somewhere inside her. Thank God, she was going to be all right. Thank God.

"Fynn, is the Princess all right?" Anna whispered.

"She's fine," I answered. I didn't know if she was all right or not.

"She was stuck up the tree and couldn't get down—I slipped," said Anna.

"She's all right."

"She was very frightened. She's only a baby kitten."

"She's fine, she's all right. You rest. I'll stay with you. Don't be frightened," I said to Anna.

"Ain't frightened, Fynn. I ain't frightened."

"Go to sleep, Tich. Have a little sleep, I've got you."

Her eyes closed and she slept. It was going to be all right. I knew it deep down inside. For two days this feeling that it was going to be all right grew and took over my fears. Her grin and her excited conversations about Mister God made me doubly sure. The knots inside me were coming undone. I was looking out of the window when she called me.

"Fynn!"

"Here, Tich. What d'you want?" I crossed to her.

"Fynn, it is like turning inside out!" There was a look of amazement on her face.

An ice-cold hand gripped my heart and squeezed hard. I remembered Granny Harding.

"Tich," my voice was too loud, "Tich, look at me!"

Her eyes flickered and her smile spread. I hurried to the window and flung it up. Cory was there.

"Get the doctor quickly," I said.

She nodded, turned on her heels and ran. Suddenly I knew what was going to happen. I went back to Anna. It wasn't time for crying, it was never time for crying. The cold dread in my heart had frozen the tears within me. I held Anna's hand. My head pounded with the idea that "whatever you shall ask in my name. . . ." I asked. I pleaded.

182

"Fynn," she whispered, and the smile lit up her face, "Fynn, I love you."

"I love you too, Tich."

"Fynn, I bet Mister God lets me get into heaven for this."

"You betcha. I bet he's waiting for you."

I wanted to say more, a whole lot more, but she wasn't listening anymore, just smiling.

The days burnt up like giant candles, and time melted, ran, and congealed into useless and hideous lumps.

Two days after the funeral I found Anna's seed pouch. It gave me something to do. I went to the cemetery and stayed for a little while. It just made things worse, that much more empty. If only I had been nearer at the time— if only I had known what she was doing, if only—if only. I tipped the seeds on the freshly turned earth and hurled the pouch from me in misery.

I wanted to hate God, wanted him out of my system, but he wouldn't go. I found God more real, more strangely real than ever before. Hate wouldn't come, but I despised him. God was an idiot, a cretin, a moron. He could have saved Anna, but he didn't; he just let this most stupid of all things happen. This child, this beautiful child, had been cut off—cut off and not yet eight. Just when she was——Hell!

The war years took me out of the East End. The war dragged its bloody boots over the face of the world until the madness was over. Thousands of other children had died; thousands more were maimed and homeless. The madness of war became the madness of victory. Victory? I got good and drunk on VJ night. It was a good way out.

I had been given a bundle of books sometime previously, but I hadn't bothered to undo them. There didn't seem much point. It was one of those idle moments; I didn't know what to do with myself. Those years had made my eyes tired with looking and my ears ache with listening. Some sign, some vision, just for a moment. I picked up the books. They didn't seem all that interesting. Nothing seemed very interesting. I flipped through the pages. It wasn't until my eyes fell upon the name of Coleridge that I stopped the pages of the book slipping through my fingers. For me Coleridge is at the top of the heap. I began to read:

"I adopt with full faith the theory of Aristotle that poetry as poetry is essentially ideal, that it avoids and excludes all accident, that its. . . ."

I turned back a few pages and began to read again. Out of the pages of that book Old Woody appeared.

"The process by which the poetic imagination works is illustrated by Coleridge from the following lines of Sir John Davies:

Thus doth she, when from individual states
She doth abstract the universal kinds,
Which then reclothed in divers names and fates,
Steal access thro' our senses to our minds."

The smoky fires of the nighttime people came drifting through my imagination: Old Woody, Convict Bill, Old Lil, Anna, and me. A few lines further on my eye caught one word, *violence.*

"The young poet," says Goethe, "must do some sort of violence to himself to get out of the mere general idea. No doubt this is difficult, but it is the very art of living."

It slowly began to make sense; the bits began to fall into place. Something was happening and it made me cry; for the first time in a long, long time I cried. I went out into the night and stayed out. The clouds seemed to be rolling back. It kept nagging at the back of my mind. Anna's life hadn't been cut short; far from it; it had been full, completely fulfilled.

The next day I headed back to the cemetery. It took me a long time to find Anna's grave. It was tucked away at the back of the cemetery. I knew that it had no head-stone, just a simple wooden cross with the name on it, "Anna." I found it after about an hour.

I had gone there with this feeling of peace inside me, as if the book had been closed, as if the story had been one of triumph, but I hadn't expected this. I stopped and gasped. This was it. The little cross leaned drunkenly, its paint peeling off, and there was the name: A N N A.

I wanted to laugh, but you don't laugh in a cemetery, do you? Not only did I want to laugh, I had to laugh. It wouldn't stay bottled up. I laughed till the tears ran down my face. I pulled up the little cross and threw it into a thicket.

"OK, Mister God," I laughed, "I'm convinced. Good old Mister God. You might be a bit slow at times, but you certainly make it all right in the end."

Anna's grave was a brilliant red carpet of poppies. Lupines stood guard in the background. A couple of trees whispered to each other while a family of little mice scurried backward and forward through the uncut grass. Anna was truly home. She didn't need a marker. You couldn't better this with a squillion tons of marble. I stayed for a little while and said good-bye to her for the first time in five years.

As I made my way back to the main gates I passed by hordes of little marble cherubs, angels, and pearly gates. I stopped in front of the twelve-foot angel, still trying to lay down its bunch of marble flowers after God knows how many years.

"Hi, chum," I said, saluting the angel, "you'll never make it, you know."

I swung on the iron gates as I yelled back into the cemetery.

"The answer is 'In my middle.' "

A finger of thrill went down my spine and I thought I heard her voice saying, "What's that the answer to, Fynn?"

"That's easy. The question is 'Where's Anna?' "

I had found her again—found her in my middle.

I felt sure that somewhere Anna and Mister God were laughing.

WHEN I SHALL DIE

by

ANNA

When I shall die,
I shall do it myself.
Nobody shall do it for me.
When I am redy,
I shall say,
'Fin, stand me up,'
and I shall look
and lagh merry.
If I fall down,
I shall be dead.